# Poems and Ballads.

# POEMS AND BALLADS

BY

GERALD MASSEY,

CONTAINING THE

## BALLAD OF BABE CHRISTABEL.

PRINTED FROM THE THIRD LONDON EDITION,

WITH

Several New Poems Never Before Published.

---

Revised and Corrected by the Author.

---

NEW YORK:
J. C. DERBY, 119 NASSAU STREET.
BOSTON:
PHILLIPS, SAMPSON & CO.
CINCINNATI:
H. W. DERBY.
1854.

# Contents.

# Preface

TO THE

# THIRD EDITION.

---

I DO not like to write a Preface. I do not think a volume of verse should need one. But, as my Book has reached a Third Edition, and as almost as much has been said about myself as about my Book, perhaps I may be excused, even by the Preface-hater, if I do take this opportunity of saying a few words. I have been considerably censured for the political opinions which it contains—as I expected to be. Before printing, I was advised not to include the political pieces, as, it was urged, they would prove an obstacle to the success of my Poetry, and close the drawing-room door against me. And if I had looked on the success of my Book in a poetical light alone, I should not have printed the greater portion of the political verses. But that was not the sole point of view. Those verses do not express what I think and feel now, since they were written some five or six years ago: yet they express what I thought and felt then, and what thousands beside me have thought and felt, and what thousands still think and feel. They were the outcome of a peculiar and marked experience. I printed the "Memoir," so that they might be read in the light, or gloom, of that experience, and the Book contain its own excuse. They have not read me aright, who have not so interpreted it. I have been blamed for the rebellious feelings to which the political pieces give utterance; but they were perfectly natural under the circumstances. Indeed, I look upon those same rebellious feelings as my very deliverance from a fatal slough. There are conditions in which many of the poor exist, where humanity must be either rebel or slave. For the slave, degradation and moral death are certain; but for the rebel there is always a chance of becoming conqueror; and the force to resist is far better than the faculty to succumb.

"It is not," says he, "that I seek to sow dissension between class and class, or fling firebrands among the combustibles of society; for when I smite the hearts of my fellows, I would rather they should gush with the healing waters of love, than with the fearful fires of hatred. I yearn to raise them into loveable beings. I would kindle in the hearts of the masses a sense of the beauty and grandeur of the universe, call forth the lineaments of Divinity in their poor worn faces, give them glimpses of the grace and glory of Love and the marvellous significance of Life, and elevate the standard of Humanity for all. But strange wrongs are daily done in the land, bitter feelings are felt, and wild words will be spoken. It was not for myself alone that I wrote these things: it was always the condition of others that so often made the mist rise up and cloud my vision. Nor was it for myself that I have uncurtained some scenes of my life to the public gaze, but as an illustration of the lives of others, who suffer and toil on, 'die, and make no sign;' and because one's own personal experience is of more value than that of others taken upon hearsay."

So I keep my political verses as memorials of my past, as one might keep some worn-out garment because he had passed through the furnace in it, nothing doubting that in the future they will often prove my passport to the hearts and homes of thousands of the poor, when the minstrel comes to their door with something better to bring them. They will know that I have suffered their sufferings, wept their tears, thought their thoughts, and felt their feelings; and they will trust me.

I have been congratulated by some correspondents on the

uses of suffering, and the riches I have wrung from Poverty: as though it were a blessed thing to be born in the condition in which I was, and surrounded with untoward circumstances as I have been. My experience tells me that Poverty is inimical to the development of Humanity's noblest attributes. Poverty is a never-ceasing struggle for the means of living, and it makes one hard and selfish. To be sure, noble lives have been wrought out in the sternest poverty. Many such are being wrought out now, by the unknown heroes and martyrs of the Poor. I have known men and women in the very worst circumstances, to whom heroism seemed a heritage, and to be noble a natural way of living. But they were so in spite of their poverty, not because of it. What they might have been if the world had done better by them, I cannot tell; but if their minds had been enriched by culture, the world had been the gainer. When Christ said "Blessed are they who suffer," he did not speak of those who suffer from want and hunger, and who always see the Bastile looming up and blotting out the sky of their future. Such suffering brutalizes. True natures ripen and strengthen in suffering; but it is that suffering which chastens and ennobles—that which clears the spiritual sight—not the anxiety lest work should fail, and the want of daily bread. The beauty of Suffering is not to be read in the face of Hunger.

Above all, Poverty is a cold place to write Poetry in. It is not attractive to poetical influences. The Muses do not like entertainment which is not fit for man or beast. Nor do the best fruits of Poetry ripen in the rain and shade and wind alone: they want sunshine, warmth, and the open sky. And should the heart of a poor man break into song, it is likely that his poverty may turn into hailstones that which might have fallen on the world in fructifying rain. A poor man, fighting his battle of life, has little time for the rapture of repose which Poetry demands. He cannot take Poetry, like a Bride, to his heart and home, and devote a life to her service. He can only keep some innermost chamber of his heart sacred for her, from whence he gets occasional glimpses of her wondrous beauty, when he can steal away from the outward strife, like some child who has found a treasure, and steals aside to look on it in secret and alone, lest rude and importunate companions should snatch it from the possessor's hands. Considering all things, it may appear madness for a poor man to attempt Poetry in the face of the barriers that surround him. So many hearts have been broken, so many lives have been wasted, so many lions are in the way of the Gate Beautiful, and so many wrecks lie by the path! And so it is—a diseased madness, or a divine one. If the disease, then there is no help for a man: if the divine, then there is no hinderance for him.

Who would not pity the poor versifier at the outset of his career? But who would not also rejoice with him in the end, when the world crowns him a Poet with pæans of acclaim? And, in spite of all things, there will be Poetry in the midst of poverty. Even as there is scarcely a space in the world so barren but some plot of natural richness will be running all to flowers—some type of loveliness will be starting up from Earth's inner Sea of Beauty, even in waste and wilderness, on rock and ruin, in Alpine snows and sandy solitudes—so is it with Poetry, the flower of Humanity. It will continually be springing, in its own natural way, in the most bleak and barren bye-ways of the world, as well as in the richest and most cultivated pastures. The winds of heaven, or the birds of God, will drop the seed, and the flower will follow, even though sown amid the bushes and brambles of the obscurest hamlet, or in the crevices of the city pavement. Not that the wilderness, or the rock, or the snows, are the fittest places to rear flowers of most exquisite fragrance and beauty; neither are Poverty and Penury, with their hell of torture, and daily wrestle with grim Death, the fittest soil to grow and perfect the flower of Poetry. The greatest original Genius can only develop itself according to the circumstances which environ it. It needs food to nourish it, and time and opportunity to unfold it. If it lack these, it must remain dwarfed and stunted, and perhaps wither and die.

Besides, it is not while the fight is raging, and the struggle is sore, that the Poet can sing. He must first do battle and overcome, climb from the stir and strife, and be able to watch from his mountain where he dwells apart. The fullest and rarest streams of Poetry only flow through a mind at peace. The mirror of the Poet's soul must be calm and clear: else it will give forth distorted reflections and false imaginings.

Had I known, when I began to write verses, what I know now, I think I should have been intimidated, and not have begun at all. So many and so glorious are the luminaries already up and shining, that one would pause before hoisting a rushlight. But I was ignorant of these things. And as I have begun, and conquered some preliminary difficulties,—as I have been sweated down to the proper jockey-weight at which I can ride Pegasus with little danger of spraining his wings,—and as a purpose has gradually and unconsciously grown upon me, I dare say I shall go on, making the best of my limited materials, with the view of writing some songs that may become dear to the hearts of the people, cheering them in their sorrows, voicing their aspirations, lighting them on the way up which they are groping darkly after better things, and saluting their triumphs with hymns of victory!

I cannot conclude without thanking those Critics who have given me so generous a welcome. And I would also thank those who have not spared my faults, or dwelt tenderly on my failings. They, also, have done me good, and I am grateful for it. Friendly praise is somewhat like a warm bath,—apt to enervate, especially if we stay in too long; but friendly censure is like a cold bath, bracing and healthful, though we are always glad to get out of it. Some of the Critics have called me a "Poet;" but that word is much too lightly spoken, much too freely bandied about. I know what a Poet is too well to fancy that I am one yet. It is a high standard that I set up myself, and I do not ask it to be lowered to reach my stature; nor would I have the Poet's awful crown diminished to mete my lesser brow. I may have that something within which kindles flame-like at the breath of Love, or mounts into song in the presence of Beauty; but alas! mine is a "jarring lyre." If I were a Critic, I should be savagely severe on this subject. The dearth of Poetry should be great in a country where we hail as Poets such as have been crowned of late.

For myself, I have only entered the lists, and inscribed my name: the race has yet to be run. Whether I shall run it, and win the Poet's crown, or not, time alone will prove, and not the prediction of friend or foe. The crowns of Poetry are not in the keeping of Critics. There have been many who have given some sign of promise,—just set a rainbow of hope in the dark cloud of their life,—and never fulfilled their promise; and the world has wondered why. But it might not have been matter of wonder if the world could have read what was written behind the cloud. Others, again, are songful in youth, like the nightingales in Spring, who soon cease to sing, because they have to build nests, rear their young, and provide for them; and so the songs grow silent,—the heart is full of cares, and the dreamer has no time to dream. I hope that my future holds some happier fate. I think there is a work for me to do, and I trust to accomplish it.

GERALD MASSEY.

*April*, 1854.

# A Biographic Sketch.

---

The reader of the miscellaneous literature of the day has doubtless met with the name of Gerald Massey attached to poems strikingly beautiful in language and intensely passionate in feeling. These poems have heretofore been published chiefly in journals which are yet in a great measure *tabooed* in what are regarded as "respectable literary circles." The "Spirit of Freedom," a cheap journal, started in 1849, and written exclusively by working-men, contained a large number of them ; and others have since appeared in the "Christian Socialist," a cheap journal conducted by Clergymen of the Church of England ; and many others also, of great beauty, have been published in the "Leader," a remarkably able journal conducted by Thornton Hunt, the son of the poet.

You see at once that the writer is a man of vivid genius, and is full of the true poetic fire. Some of his earlier pieces are indignant expostulations with society at the wrongs of suffering humanity ; passionate protests against those hideous disparities of life which meet our eye on every side ; against power wrongfully used ; against fraud and oppression in their more rampant forms ; mingled with appeals to the higher influences of knowledge, justice, mercy, truth, and love. It is always thus with the poet who has worked his way to the light through darkness, suffering, and toil. Give a poor down-trodden man culture, and, in nine cases out of ten, you only increase his sensitiveness to pain : you agonize him with the sight of pleasures which are to him forbidden ; you quicken his sense of despair at the frightful inequalities of the human lot. There are thousands of noble natures, with minds which, under better circumstances, would have blessed and glorified their race, who have been for ever blasted—crushed into the mire—or condemned to courses of desperate guilt !—for one who, like Gerald Massey, has nobly risen above his trials and temptations, and triumphed over them. And when such a man does find a voice, surely "rose-water" verses and "hot-pressed" sonnets are not to be expected of him : such things are not by any means the natural products of a life of desperate struggling with poverty. When the self-risen and self-educated man speaks and writes now-a-days, it is of the subjects nearest to his heart. Literature is not a mere intelligent epicurism with men who have suffered and grown wise, but a real, earnest, passionate, vehement, living thing—a power to move others, a means to elevate themselves, and to emancipate their order. This is a marked peculiarity of our times; knowledge is now more than ever regarded as a power to elevate, not merely individuals, but classes. Hence the most intelligent of working-men at this day are intensely political: we merely state this as a *fact* not to be disputed. In former times, when literature was regarded mainly in the light of a rich man's luxury, poets who rose out of the working-class sung as their patrons wished. Bloomfield and Clare sang of the quiet beauty of rural life, and painted pictures of evening skies, purling brooks, and grassy meads. Burns could with difficulty repress the "Jacobin" spirit which burned within him; and yet even he was rarely, if ever, political in his tone. His strongest verses, having a political bearing, were those addressed to the Scotch Representatives in reference to the Excise regulations as to the distillation of whiskey. But come down to our own day, and mark the difference: Elliot, Nichol, Bamford, the author of "Ernest," the Chartist Epic, Davisthe "Belfast Man," De Jean, Massey, and many others, are intensely political; and they defend themselves for their selection of subjects as Elliot did, when he said, "Poetry is impassioned truth; and why should we not utter it in the shape that touches our condition the mostly closely—the political?" But how it happens that the writings of working-men now-a-days so generally assume the political tone, will be best ascertained from the following sketch of the life of Gerald Massey:—

He was born in May, 1828, and is, therefore, barely twenty-five years of age. He first saw the light in a little stone hut near Tring, in Herts, one of those miserable abodes in which so many of our happy peasantry—their country's pride!—are condemned to live and die. One shilling a week was the rent of this hovel, the roof of which was so low that a man could not stand upright in it. Massey's father was, and still is, a canal boatman, earning the wage of ten shillings a week. Like most other peasants in this "highly-favoured Christian country," he has had no opportunities of education, and never could write his own name. But Gerald Massey was blessed in his mother, from whom he derived a finely-organized brain and a susceptible temperament. Though quite illiterate, like her husband, she had a firm, free spirit—it's broken now!—a tender yet courageous heart, and a pride of honest poverty which she never ceased to cherish.. But she needed all her strength and courage to bear up under the privations of her lot. Sometimes the husband fell out of work; and there was no bread in the cupboard, except what was purchased by the labour of the elder children, some of whom were early sent to work in the neighbouring silk-mill. Disease, too, often fell upon the family, cooped up in that unwholesome hovel: indeed, the wonder is, not that our peasantry should be diseased, and grow old and haggard before their time, but that they should exist at all in such lazar-houses and cesspools.

None of the children of this poor family were educated,

in the common acceptance of the term. Several of them were sent for a short time to a penny school, where the teacher and the taught were about on a par ; but so soon as they were of age to work, the children were sent to the silk-mill. The poor cannot afford to keep their children at school, if they are of an age to work and earn money. They must help to eke out their parents' slender gains, even though it be only by a few pence weekly. So, at eight years of age, Gerald Massey went into the silk-manufactory, rising at five o'clock in the morning, and toiling there till half-past six in the evening ; up in the grey dawn, or in the winter before the daylight, and trudging to the factory through the wind or in the snow ; seeing the sun only through the factory windows ; breathing an atmosphere laden with rank oily vapour, his ears deafened by the roar of incessant wheels ;—

> "Still all the day the iron wheels go onward,
> Grinding life down from its mark ;
> And the children's souls, which God is calling sunward,
> Spin on blindly in the dark."

What a life for a child ! What a substitute for tender prattle, for childish glee, for youthful playtime ! Then home shivering under the cold, starless sky, on Saturday nights, with 9*d.*, 1*s.*, or 1*s.* 3*d.*, for the whole week's work ; for such were the respective amounts of the wages earned by the child labour of Gerald Massey.

But the mill was burned down, and the children held jubilee over it. The boy stood for twelve hours in the wind, and sleet, and mud, rejoicing in the conflagration which thus liberated him. Who can wonder at this? Then he went to straw-plaiting,—as toilsome, and perhaps, more unwholesome than factory work. Without exercise, in a marshy district, the plaiters were constantly having racking attacks of ague. The boy had the disease for three years, ending with tertian ague. Sometimes four of the family, and the mother, lay ill at one time, all crying with thirst, with no one to give them drink, and each too weak to help the other. How little do we know of the sufferings endured by the poor and struggling classes of our population, especially in our rural districts! No press echoes their wants, or records their sufferings; and they live almost as unknown to us as if they were the inhabitants of some undiscovered country.

And now take, as an illustration, the child-life of Gerald Massey. "Having had to earn my own dear bread," he says, "by the eternal cheapening of flesh and blood thus early, I never knew what childhood meant. I had no childhood. Ever since I can remember, I have had the aching fear of want, throbbing heart and brow The currents of my life were early poisoned, and few, methinks, would pass unscathed through the scenes and circumstances in which I have lived; none, if they were as curious and precocious as I was. The child comes into the world like a new coin with the stamp of God upon it;

and in like manner as the Jews sweat down sovereigns, by hustling them in a bag to get gold-dust out them, so is the poor man's child hustled and sweated down in this bag of society to get wealth out of it ; and even as the impress of the Queen is effaced by the Jewish process, so is the image of God worn from heart and brow, and day by day the child recedes devil-ward. I look back now with wonder, not that so few escape, but that any escape at all, to win a nobler growth for their humanity. So blighting are the influences which surround thousands in early life, to which I can bear such bitter testimony."

And how fared the growth of this child's mind the while? Thanks to the care of his mother, who had sent him to the penny school, he had learnt to read, and the desire to read had been awakened. Books, however, were very scarce. The Bible and Bunyan were the principal ; he committed many chapters of the former to memory, and accepted all Bunyan's allegory as *bonâ fide* history. Afterwards he obtained access to "Robinson Crusoe" and a few Wesleyan tracts left at the cottage. These constituted his sole reading, until he came up to London, at the age of fifteen, as an errand-boy ; and now, for the first time in his life, he met with plenty of books, reading all that came in his way, from "Lloyd's Penny Times," to Cobbett's Works, "French without a Master," together with English, Roman, and Grecian history. A ravishing awakenment ensued,—the delightful sense of growing knowledge,—the charm of new thought,—the wonders of a new world.

"Till then," he says, "I had often wondered why I lived at all,—whether

'It was not better not to be,
I was so full of misery.'

Now I began to think that the crown of all desire, and the sum of all existence, was to read and get knowledge. Read ! read ! read ! I used to read at all possible times, and in all possible places ; up in bed till two or three in the morning,—nothing daunted by once setting the bed on fire. Greatly indebted was I also to the bookstalls, where I have read a great deal, often folding a leaf in a book, and returning the next day to continue the subject ; but sometimes the book was gone, and then great was my grief ! When out of a situation, I have often gone without a meal to purchase a book. Until I fell in love, and began to rhyme as a matter of consequence, I never had the least predilection for poetry. In fact, I always eschewed it ; if I ever met with any, I instantly skipped it over, and passed on, as one does with the description of scenery, &c., in a novel. I always loved the birds and flowers, the woods and the stars ; I felt delight in being alone in a summer-wood, with song, like a spirit, in the trees, and the golden sun-bursts glinting through the verdurous roof ; and was conscious of a mysterious creeping of the blood, and tingling of the nerves, when standing alone in the starry midnight, as in God's own presence-chamber. But until I began to rhyme, I cared nothing for written poetry. The first verses I ever made were upon 'Hope,' when I was utterly hopeless ; and after I had begun, I never ceased for about four years, at the end of which time I rushed into print."

There was, of course, crudeness both of thought and expression in the first verses of the poet, which were published in a provincial paper. But there were nerve, rhythm, and poetry ; the burthen of the song was, " At eventime it shall be light." The leading idea of the poem was the power of knowledge, virtue, and temperance, to elevate the condition of the poor,—a noble idea, truly. Shortly after he was encouraged to print a shilling volume of " Poems and Chansons," in his native town of Tring, of which some 250 copies were sold. Of his latter poems we shall afterwards speak.

But a new power was now working upon his nature, as might have been expected,—the power of opinion, as expressed in books, and in the discussions of his fellow-workers.

" As an errand-boy," he says, " I had of course, many hardships to undergo, and to bear with much tyranny ; and that led me into reasoning upon men and things, the causes of misery, the anomalies of our societary state, politics, &c., and the circle of my being rapidly out-surged. New power came to me with all that I saw, and thought, and read. I studied political works,—such as Paine, Volney, Howitt, Louis Blanc, &c., which gave me another element to mould into my verse, though I am convinced that a poet must sacrifice much if he write party-political poetry. His politics must be above the pinnacle of party zeal; the politics of eternal truth, right, and justice. He must not waste a life on what to-morrow may prove to have been merely the question of a day. The French Revolution of 1848 had the greatest effect on me of any circumstance connected with my own life. It was scarred and blood-burnt into the very core of my being. This little volume of mine is the fruit thereof."

But, meanwhile, he had been engaged in other literary work. Full of new thoughts, and bursting with aspirations of freedom, he started, in April, 1849, a cheap journal, written entirely by working-men, entitled, "The Spirit of Freedom:" it was full of fiery earnestness, and half of its weekly contents were supplied by Gerald Massey himself, who acted as editor. It cost him five situations during the period of eleven months,—twice because he was detected burning candle far on into the night, and three times because of the tone of the opinions to which he gave utterance. The French Revolution of 1848 having, amongst its other issues, kindled the zeal of the working-men in this country in the cause of association, Gerald Massey eagerly joined them, and he has been recently instrumental in giving some impetus to that praiseworthy movement,—the object of which is to permanently elevate the condition of the producing classes, by advancing them to the status of capitalists as well as labourers.

A word or two as to Gerald Massey's recent poetry. Bear in mind that he is yet but a youth ;—at twenty-three a man can scarcely be said fairly to have entered his manhood ; and yet, if we except Robert Nichol, who died at twenty-four, we know of no English poet of his class, who has done any thing to compare with him. Some of his most beautiful pieces originally appeared in the columns of the "Leader." They give you the idea of a practised hand—one who has reached the full prime of his poetic manhood. Take, for instance, his "Lyrics of Love," so full of beauty and tenderness. Nor are his "Songs of Progress" less full of poetic power and beauty.

Gerald Massey is a teacher through the heart. He is familiar with the passions, and leans towards the tender and loving aspect of our nature. He takes after Burns more than after Wordsworth, Elliot rather than Thomson. He is but a young man, though he has had crowded into his twenty-three years already the life of an old man. He has won his experience in the school of the poor, and nobly earned his title to speak to them as a man and a brother, dowered with "the hate of hate, the scorn of scorn, the love of Love."—*Extract from an article in "Eliza Cook's Journal,"* 1581, *written by Dr. Samuel Smiles.*

# Poems and Ballads.

## TO MY WIFE.

Like those Ambassadors of old, that went
To the far Orient land, with kingly gifts
Of Gold, so royal-rare and wondrous fine;
And Jewels—from which a subtle spirit lookt—
To nestle richly between Beauty's breasts—
And crown her gorgeous brows with winking flame,
Or clothe her starrily as Queenly Night,
And found that land a garden where they grew,
Lavish, as all the dews were turn'd to gems;
So bring I thee, Sweet Lady of my love,
My gems, which I have garner'd up, to find
How poor they are beside thy peerless wealth.
Th' Elysium where thy tender spirit dwells
Is written o'er with thoughts of beauty, thick
As starry mysteries written on the night.
Thy realm is rich in Memory's golden mines,

And flashing out with harvest-fields of Hope.
My Muse! that moveth swathed with holier light,
Throned on the regnant heights of Womanhood
In all thy summer beauty, warm as when
I lookt out on the sunny side of Life,
And saw thee summering like a blooming Vine,
That reacheth globes of wine in at the lattice
By the ripe armful, with ambrosial smile.
The flying Cares but touch thy Life's fair face,
Lightly as swimming shadows dusk the Lake.
Come sit thee down, dear, by my side, To-night;
The world shut out, our little world shut in!
Where we are happy as the Bird whose nest
Is heaven'd in the heart of purple Hills,
Or region'd in the palmy top of life,
Where sleep is dark and lusty as leaves in June:
Now shut thine eyes, and see a pageant bloom
Upon the dark,—a Vision sweeping by.
I was a dweller amid shadows grim:
Till FREEDOM toucht my yearning eyes, and lo!
Life in a shining circle, rounding rose,
As heaven on heaven goes up the jewell'd night.
New floods of passionate life swirl'd at my heart,
Like Ocean-surges rolling round the world:
And FREEDOM was my glittering Bride. For me
She walkt the world as a Divinity,
Sang like a Spirit in Life's darken'd ways,
I' the Rainbow reacht forth girdling arms of love,

To clasp the Unapparent to the Earth,—
Turn'd common things to beauty : as the sun
Doth kindle glory in the grass and dust—
When forth flame-plumed in chariot sublime,
And rode the winds, like him who walks the worlds
When the roused Storm-God strode his War-Horse, Ocean,
That sloughs the foam, with flying mane of fire!
And when the fresh Morn flower'd like a Rose,
Birds sang of her, and all their happy hearts
Rang out in music, Leaves clapt faery hands,
The Flowers for joy stood tearful in her glory,
And World went singing, unto World, of FREEDOM.
And I would blazon her melodious name,
Sing some wild pæan should touch the world to tears,
Or chariot it to battle in her Cause :
For O! her softest breath, that might not stir
The summer gossamer tremulous on its throne,
Makes the crown'd Tyrants start with realmless looks!
I would have given the lustre of my life
To add one jewel to her Diadem!
And then thou cam'st, and LOVE grew lord of all.
Look how the Sun puts out the eyes of fire!
So when LOVE's royal glance my lattice lit,
The fires of FREEDOM whiten'd on my hearth.
The sleeping Beauty in my heart's charm'd Palace
Woke at Love's kiss. My life was set aflush,
As Roses redden when the Spring moves by,
And the green buds peer out like eyes, to see

The delicate Spirit whose sweet presence stirr'd them.
How my heart ripen'd in its flooding spring ;
As when the sap runs up the tingling trees,
Till all the sunny life laughs out in leaves,
And lifts its fluttering wings ! So my heart felt
With such brave shoots of glory bursting up,
As it had flower'd for Immortality.
The heights of Being came out from their cloud,
As the cliffs kindle when the Morning comes
Swimming the utmost sea in ruddy haste,
With foam of glory ; and the ruby light,
Like mellow wine, runs down remotest hills.
Thou cam'st, my sparking Bird of Paradise !
With a soft murmuring as of winnowing wings
That fold the nest so Dove-like tenderly !
With brows that parted lovely waves of hair,
And took the gazer's eye like some white Grace !
Eyes, loving large ! Lips Houri-like, that light
A soul to glory with their kiss of fire ;
And cheeks fresh-misted with the bloom of Morn.
And thou didst move, a Splendour mid Life's Shadows,
Making a Rembrandt Picture. So the Stars
In all their glory pass the shrinking Dark.
O, I was stirr'd as though a Spirit went by ;
Or I had met some awful Loveliness,
That haunts the realm of Dreams, or duskly floats
Across the wandering solitudes of Thought.
So Love was lord of all. I touch my lyre,

And love o'erflows my heart, and floods my hand.
Love makes all dear delights so soothly sweet,
Life pants heart-stifled with its luscious load,
Like young Earth claspt in June's voluptuous arms,
Faint with her fragrance, flooded up in flowers.
Love's life divine, and Beauty is its smile.
O Love will make the killing crown of thorn
Burst into blossom on the Martyr's brow !
Upon Love's bosom Earth floats like an Ark
Safely through all the Deluge of the dark.
Love rays us round as glory swathes a star,
And, from the mystic touch of lips and palms,
Streams rosy warmth enough t' illume a world :
And Spirit-eyes, from out the purpling glooms,
Mark how we feed this human Altar-flame,
How speeds this ripening intc Diety !
What glittering robes for immortality
Trail starry radiance through our night of Earth !
And in our home thy presence maketh Love
A Mortal, who hath died to rise again,
Immortal, in its nobler life with thee.
O Love ! sublime me unto loftier things ;
Roll up my Orb from Passion's misting Deep,
To climb the heights of Thought's eternal Vast ;
And though it shine not mid the Suns of Song,
To set a World sweet-murmuring in its light,
Like Memnon at the radiant touch of Dawn,
I know each Star hath its own perfect place

In heaven, though it may have no name on Earth.
I hope my hope, and dream my dream that life
With me shall yet ring out melodious, 'twixt
The silences of heaven and the grave.
O Labour ! blind and feeling for the day !
Might I go forth to peer with eagle ken
Into the blessed land of promise, where
The Future like a fruitfuller Summer sits
Ripening Her Eden silently, to bear
The crowning flower of consummated Life,—
Where Freedom's Song-Birds fly, to build their nests,
And warm to life their brood of darling dreams :
Then see thy dark face lighten at my news,
And hearten thee to lift up grander brows
With light o'erflowing like a shining Sea.
I see a shape behind a mist, that burns
I' the flushing distance of some unseen Goal ;
That grows with gazing on, like Lovers' beauty.
With beckoning smiles the Glory draws me on ;
One hand points up, one holds a glittering crown,
For me to climb and wear with lordlier growth,
And airy Voices call me, bid me leap
In Victory's Car as it goes bickering by.
And Thou, dear Wife ! with exultation lit,
Wilt weep proud tears t' enrich my wine of joy,—
A costlier cup than ever Anthony's Queen
Magnificent ! drank in her voluptuous vein !

## THE BALLAD OF BABE CHRISTABEL.

WHEN Danaë-Earth bares all her charms,
And gives the God her perfect flower,
Who in the sunshine's golden shower,
Leaps warm into her amorous arms!

When buds are bursting on the brier,
And all the kindled greenery glows,
And life hath richest overflows,
And morning fields are fringed with fire:

When young Maids feel Love stir i' the blood,
And wanton with the kissing leaves
And branches, and the quick sap heaves,
And dances to a ripen'd flood;

Till, blown to its hidden heart with sighs,
Love's red rose burns i' the cheek so dear,
And, as sea-jewels upward peer,
Love-thoughts melt through their swimming eyes:

When Beauty walks in bravest dress,
And, fed with April's mellow showers,
The earth laughs out with sweet May-flowers
That flush for very happiness:

And Spider-Puck such wonder weaves
    O' nights, and nooks of greening gloom
    Are rich with violets that bloom
In the cool dark of dewy leaves :

When Rose-buds drink the fiery wine
    Of Dawn, with crimson stains i' the mouth,
    All thirstily as yearning Youth
From Love's hand drinks the draught divine ;

And honey'd plots are drowsed with Bees :
    And Larks rain music by the shower,
    While singing, singing hour by hour,
Song like a Spirit sits i' the Trees !

When fainting hearts forget their fears
    And in the poorest Life's salt cup
    Some rare wine runs, and Hope builds up
Her rainbow over Memory's tears !

It fell upon a merry May morn,
    I' the perfect prime of that sweet time
    When daisies whiten, woodbines climb,—
The dear Babe Christabel was born.

All night the Stars bright watches kept,
    Like Gods that look a golden calm ;
    The Silence dropt its precious balm,
And the tired world serenely slept.

The birds were darkling in the nest,
    Or bosom'd in voluptuous trees :
    On beds of flowers the panting breeze
Had kist its fill and sank to rest.

All night beneath the Cottage eaves,
    A lonely light, with tremulous Arc,
    Surged back a space the sea of dark,
And glanced among the glimmering leaves.

Without ! the quiet heavens above
    The nest of life, did lean and brood !
    Within ! the Mother's tears of blood
Wet the Gethsemane of her love !

And when the Morn with frolic zest,
    Lookt through the curtains of the night,
    There was a dearer dawn of light,
A tenderer life the Mother's prest !

Ah! bliss to make the brain reel wild!
    The Star new-kindled in the dark—
    Life that had fluttered like a Lark—
Lay in her bosom a sweet Child!

How she had felt it drawing down
    Her nesting heart more close and close,—
    Her rose-bud ripening to a Rose,
That she should one day see full-blown!

How she had throbb'd with hopes and fears,
    And strain'd her inner eyes till dim,
    To see the coming glory swim
Through the rich mist of happy tears;

For it, her woman's heart drank up
    And smiled at, Sorrow's darkest dole:
    And now Delight's most dainty soul
Was crusht for her in one rich cup!

And then delicious languors crept,
    Like nectar, on her pain's hot drouth,
    And feeling fingers—kissing mouth—
Being faint with joy, the mother slept.

BABE Christabel was royally born !
For when the earth was flusht with flowers,
And drencht with beauty in rainbow showers,
She came through golden gates of Morn.

No chamber arras-pictured round,
Where sunbeams golden gorgeous gloom,
And touch its glories into bloom,
And footsteps fell withouten sound,

Was her Birth-place that merry May-morn ;
No gifts were heapt, no bells were rung,
No healths were crown'd, no songs were sung,
When dear Babe Christabel was born :

But Nature on the darling smiled,
And with her beauty's blessing crown'd :
Love brooded o'er the hallowed ground,
And there were Angels with the Child !

And May her kisses of love did blow
On amorous airs, that came to her
With gifts of Frankincense and Myrrh,
As came the Magi long ago

To worship Bethlehem's baby-King,
    Spring-Birds make welcoming merriment,
    And all the Flowers for welcome sent
The secret sweetness of the Spring.

With glancing lights and shimmering shade,
    And cheeks that toucht and ripelier burn'd
    May-Roses in at the lattice yearn'd
A-tiptoe, and Good Morrow bade.

No purple and fine linen might
    Be hoarded up for her sweet sake :
    But Mother's love shall clothe and make
The little wearer richly dight !

Wide worlds of worship are their eyes,
    Their loyal hearts are worlds of love,
    Who fondly clasp the stranger Dove,
And read its news from Paradise.

Their looks praise God—souls sing for glee :
    They think if this old world had toil'd
    Through ages to bring forth their child,
It hath a glorious destiny.

O HAPPY Husband ! happy Wife !
The rarest blessing Heaven drops down,
The sweetest blossom in Spring's crown,
Starts in the furrows of your life !

God ! what a towering height ye win,
Who cry, " Lo my beloved Child !"
And, life on life sublimely piled,
Ye touch the heavens and peep within !

Look how a star of glory swims
Down aching silences of space,
Flushing the Darkness till its face
With beating heart of light o'erbrims !

So brightening came Babe Christabel,
To touch the earth with fresh romance,
And light a Mother's countenance
With looking on her miracle.

With hands so flower-like soft, and fair,
She caught at life, with words as sweet
As first spring violets, and feet
As faery-light as feet of air.

The Father, down in Toil's mirk mine,
    Turns to his wealthy world above,
    Its radiance, and its home of love ;
And lights his life like sun-struck wine.

The Mother moves with queenlier tread :
    Proud swell the globes of ripe delight
    Above her heart, so warm and white
A pillow for the baby-head !

Their natures deepen, well-like clear,
    Till God's eternal stars are seen,
    For ever shining and serene,
By eyes anointed Beauty's seer.

A sense of glory all things took,—
    The red Rose-Heart of Dawn would blow,
    And Sundown's sumptuous pictures show
Babe-Cherubs wearing their Babe's look !

And round their peerless one they clung,
    Like bees about a flower's wine-cup :
    New thoughts and feelings blossom'd up,
And hearts for very fulness sung.

Of what their budding Babe should grow,
    When the Maid crimson'd into Wife,
    And crown'd the summit of some life,
Like Phosphor, with morn on its brow !

And they should bless her for a Bride,
    Who, like a splendid saint alit
    In some heart's seventh heaven, should sit,
As now in theirs, all glorified !

But O ! 't was all too white a brow
    To flush with Passion that doth fire
    With Hymen's torch its own death-pyre,—
So pure her heart was beating now !

And thus they built their Castles brave
    In fairy lands of gorgeous cloud ;
    They never saw a little white shroud,
Nor guess'd how flowers may mask the grave.

---

She grew a sweet and sinless Child,
    In sun and shadow,—calm and strife ;
    A Rainbow on the dark of Life,
From Love's own radiant heaven down-smiled !

In lonely loveliness she grew,—
    A shape all music, light, and love,
    With startling looks, so eloquent of
The spirit burning into view.

At Childhood she could seldom play
    With merry heart, whose flashings rise
    Like splendour-wingéd butterflies
From honeyed hearts of flowers in May :

The fields with flowers flamed out and flusht,
    The Roses into crimson yearned,
    With cloudy fire the wall-flowers burn'd,
And blood-red Sunsets bloom'd and blusht—

And still her cheek was pale as pearl,—
    It took no tint of Summer's wealth
    Of colour, warmth, and wine of Health :—
Ah ! Death's hand whitely pressed the Girl !

No blushes swarm'd to the sun's kiss
    Where violet-veins ran purple light,
    So tenderly thro' Parian white
Touching you into tenderness.

A spirit-look was in her face,
    That shadow'd a miraculous range
    Of meanings, ever rich and strange
Or lighten'd glory in the place.

Such mystic lore was in her eyes,
    And light of other worlds than ours,
    She lookt as she had fed on flowers,
And drunk the dews of Paradise.

Her brow—fit home for daintiest dreams—
    With such a dawn of light was crown'd,
    And reeling ringlets showered round,
Like sunny sheaves of golden beams :

And she would talk so weirdly-wild,
    And grow upon your wonderings,
    As tho' her stature rose on wings !
And you forgot she was a Child.

Ah ! she was one of those who come
    With pledgéd promise not to stay
    Long, ere the Angels let them stray
To nestle down in earthly home :

And, thro' the windows of her eyes,
    We often saw her saintly soul,
    Serene, and sad, and beautiful,
Go sorrowing for lost Paradise.

In Earth she took no lusty root,
    Her beauty of promise to disclose,
    And round into the Woman-Rose,
And climb into Life's crowning fruit :

She came—like music in the night
    Floating as heaven in the brain,
    A moment oped, and shut again,
And all is dark where all was light.

She came,—as comes the light of smiles
    O'er earth, and every budding thing
    Makes quick with beauty—alive with Spring;
Then goeth to Hesperian Isles.

---

MIDNIGHT was trancéd solemnly
    Thinking of dawn: Her Star-thoughts burn'd!
    The Trees like burden'd Prophets yearn'd,
Rapt in a wind of prophecy:

When, like the Night, the shadow of Woe
    On all things laid its hand death-dark,
    Our last hope went out like a spark,
And a cry smote heaven like a blow!

We sat and watcht by Life's dark stream,
    Our love-lamp blown about the night,
    With hearts that lived as lived its light,
And died as died its precious gleam.

In Death's face hers flasht up and smiled,
    As smile the young flowers in their prime,
    I' the face of their grey murderer Time,
And Death for true love kist our child.

She thought our good-night kiss was given,
And like a lily her life did close ;
Angels uncurtain'd that repose,
And the next waking dawn'd in heaven.

---

WITH her white hands claspt she sleepeth ; her heart is husht, and lips are cold ;
Death shrouds up her heaven of beauty, and a weary way I go,
Like the sheep without a Shepherd on the wintry norland wold,
With the face of Day shut out by blinding snow.

O'er its widow'd nest my heart sits moaning for its young that's fled
From this world of wail and weeping, gone to join her starry peers ;
And my light of life o'ershadow'd where the dear one lieth dead,
And I'm crying in the dark with many fears.

All last night-tide she seemed near me, like a lost beloved Bird,
Beating at the lattice louder than the sobbing wind and rain ;

And I call'd across the night with tender name and fondling word;
And I yearn'd out thro' the darkness, all in vain.

Heart will plead, "Eyes cannot see her: they are blind with tears of pain;"
And it climbeth up and straineth, for dear life, to look and hark
While I call her once again: but there cometh no refrain,
And it droppeth down, and dieth in the dark.

---

In this dim world of clouding cares,
We rarely know, till wildered eyes
See white wings lessening up the skies.
The Angels with us unawares.

And thou hath stolen a jewel, Death!
Shall light thy dark up like a Star,
A Beacon kindling from afar
Our light of love, and fainting faith.

Thro' tears it gleams perpetually,
And glitters thro' the thickest glooms,
Till the eternal morning comes
To light us o'er the Jasper Sea.

With our best branch in tenderest leaf,
    We've strewn the way our Lord doth come ;
    And, ready for the harvest-home,
His Reapers bind our ripest sheaf.

Our beautiful Bird of light hath fled :
    Awhile she sat with folded wings—
    Sang round us a few hoverings—
Then straightway into glory sped.

And white-wing'd Angels nurture her :
    With heaven's white radiance robed and crown'd,
    And all Love's purple glory round,
She summers on the Hills of Myrrh.

Thro' Childhood's morning-land, serene
    She walkt betwixt us twain, like Love ;
    While, in a robe of light above,
Her better Angel walkt unseen,

Till Life's highway broke bleak and wild ;
    Then, lets her starry garments trail
    In mire, heart bleed, and courage fail,
The Angel's arms caught up the child.

Her wave of life hath backward roll'd
    To the great ocean ; on whose shore
    We wander up and down, to store
Some treasures of the times of old :

And aye we seek and hunger on
    For precious pearls and relics rare,
    Strewn on the sands for us to wear
At heart, for love of her that's gone.

O weep no more! there yet is balm
    In Gilead! Love doth ever shed
    Rich healing where it nestles,—spread
O'er desert pillows, some green Palm!

God's ichor fills the hearts that bleed;—
    The best fruit loads the broken bough;
    And in the wounds our sufferings plough,
Immortal love sows sovereign seed.

---

## LONG EXPECTED.

O MANY and many a day before we met,
I knew some spirit walkt the world alone,
Awaiting the Beloved from afar;
And I was the anointed chosen one
Of all the world to crown her queenly brows
With the imperial crown of human love,
And light its glory in her happy eyes.
I saw not with mine eyes so full of tears,
But heard Faith's low sweet singing in the night,

And, groping thro' the darkness, toucht God's hand.
I knew my sunshine somewhere warm'd the world,
Tho' I trode darkling in a perilous way ;
And I should reach it in His own good time
Who sendeth sun, and dew, and love for all :
My heart might toil on blindly, but, like earth,
It kept sure footing thro' the thickest gloom.
Earth, with her thousand voices, talkt of thee !—
Sweet winds, and whispering leaves, and piping birds ;
The trickling sunlight, and the flashing dews ;
Eve's crimson air and light of twinkling gold ;
Spring's kindled greenery, and her breath of balm ;
The happy hum and stir of summer woods,
And the light dropping of the silver rain.
Thine eyes oped with their rainy lights, and laughters,
In April's tearful heaven of tender blue,
With all the changeful beauty melting thro' them,
And Dawn and Sunset ended in thy face.
And standing as in God's own presence-chamber,
When silence lay like sleep upon the world,
And it seem'd rich to die, alone with Night,
Like Moses 'neath the kisses of God's lips !
The Stars have trembled thro' the holy hush,
And smiled down tenderly, and read to me
The love hid for me in a budding breast,
Like incense folded in a young flower's heart.
Strong as a sea-swell came the wave of wings,
Strange trouble trembled thro' my inner depths,

And answering wings have sprung within my soul;
And from the dumb waste places of the dark,
A voice has breathed, "She comes!" and ebb'd again;
While all my life stood listening for thy coming.
O, I have guessed thy presence out of sight,
And felt it in the beating of my heart.
When all was dark within, sweet thoughts would come,
As starry guests come golden down the gloom
And thro' Night's lattice smile a rare delight:
While, lifted for the dear and distant Dawn,
The face of all things were a happy light,
Like those dream-smiles which are the speech of Sleep.
Thus Love lived on, and strengthen'd with the days,
Lit by its own true light within my heart,
Like a live diamond burning in the dark.
Then came there One, a mirage of the Dawn;
She swam on towards me in her sumptuous triumph,
Voluptuously upborne, like Aphrodite
Upon a meadowy swell of emerald sea.
A ripe, serene, smile-affluent graciousness
Hung like a shifting radiance on her motion,
As bickering hues upon the Dove's neck burn.
Her lip might flush a wrinkled life in bloom!
Her eyes were an omnipotence of love!
"O eyes!" I said, "if such your glories be,
Sure 'tis a warm heart feedeth ye with light!"
The silver throbbing of her laughter pulst
The air with music rich and resonant,—

As from the deep heart of a summer night,
Some bird in sudden sparklings of fine sound
Hurries its startled being into song.
And from her sumptuous wealth of golden hair
Unto the delicate pearly finger-tip,
Fresh beauty trembled from its thousand springs :
And standing in the outer porch of life,
All eager for the templed mysteries,
With a rich heart as full of fragrant love
As May's musk-roses are of morning's wine,
What marvel if I question'd not her brow,
For the flame-signet of the Hand divine,
Or gauged it for the crown of my large love ?
I plunged to clutch the pearl of her babbling beauty,
Like some swift diver in a shallow stream,
That smites his life out on its heart of stone.
Ah ! how my life did run with fire and tears !
With what a Titan-pulse my love did beat !
But she, rose-lined without,—God pity her !—
Was cold at heart as snow in last year's nest,
And struck like death into my burning brain.
My tears that rain'd out life, she froze in falling,
And wore them, jewel-like, to deck her triumph !
But love is never lost, tho' hearts run waste ;
Its tides may gush 'mid swirling, swathing deserts,
Where no green leaf drinks up the precious life :
Yet love doth evermore enrich itself,—
Its bitterest waters run some golden sands !

No star goes down but climbs in other skies ;
The rose of Sunset folds its glory up,
To burst again from out the heart of Dawn ;
And love is never lost, tho' hearts run waste,
And sorrow makes the chasten'd heart a seer ;
The deepest dark reveals the starriest hope,
And Faith can trust her heaven behind the veil.

---

## WOOED AND WON.

THE plough of Time breaks up our Eden-land,
And tramples down its fruitful flowery prime.
Yet thro' the dust of ages living shoots
O' the old immortal seed start in the furrows ;
And, where Love looketh on with glorious eye,
These quicken'd germs of everlastingness
Flower lusty, as of old in Paradise !
And blessings on the starry chance of love !
And blessings on the morn of merry May !—
That led my footsteps to your beechen bower.
Thus hangs the picture in my mind, sweet Wife !
Rich as a Millais in its tint and tone.
Nature flasht by me with her glorious shows.
The birds were singing on the blossoming boughs,
With Love's sweet mystery stirring at their hearts,

Like first spring-motions in the veins o' the flowers.
A light of green laught up the shining hills,
Which rounded through the mellowing, gloating air,
As their big hearts heaved to some heart beyond,
Or strove with inner yearnings for the crown
Of purple rondure smiling there in heaven !
The Flowers were forth in all their conquering beauty,
And, winking in their Mother Earth's old face,
Said, all her children should have happy hearts.
Deeper and deeper in the wood's green gloom
I nestled for the fever at life's core :
And thirstily my heart was drinking in
Rich overflowings of some Cushat's love ;
When, flash ! the air instinct with splendours grew,
As if the world, while on her starry journey,
Had suddenly floated in the clime of heaven.
Upon a primrose bank you sat,—a sight
To couch the old blind sorrow of my soul !
A sweet new blossom of Humanity,—
Fresh fallen from God's own home to flower on earth.
A golden burst of sunbeams glinted through
The verdurous roof's lush-leafy greenery,
And on you dropt its crown of living light.
Your eyes—half-shut, while thro' their silken eaves
Trembled the secret sweetness hid at heart—
Oped sudden at full, and wide with wonderment !
The sweetest eyes that ever drank sun for soul :
As subtly tender as a summer heaven,

Brimm'd with the beauty of a starry night !
Your face, so dewy fresh and wondrous fair,
Kindled and lighten'd as the coming God
Were labouring upward thro' its birth of fire !
The fleetest swallow-dip of a tender smile
Ran round your mouth in thrillings ; while your cheek
Dimpled, as from the arch Love's finger-print,
Out flew his signal, fluttering in a blush !
And when your voice broke up the air for music,
It smote upon my startled heart as smites
The new-born babe's first cry a mother's ear,
Yet strangely toucht some mystic memory,
And dimly seem'd some old familiar sound.
That day, with an immortalizing kiss,
You crown'd me monarch of your rich heart-world,
Which heaved a boundless sea of love, whose tides
Ran radiant pulsings thro' your rosy limbs.
How the love-lights did float up in your eyes,
Like virgin stars from violet depths of night !
Dear eyes ! all craving with Love's ache and hunger !
And all the spirit stood in your face athirst !
And from the rose-cup of your murmuring mouth
Sweetness o'erflow'd, as from a fragrant fount.
O kiss of life ! that oped our Eden-world !
The harvest of an age's wealth of bliss
In that first kiss was reapt in one rich minute !
The wanton airs came breathing like the touch
Of fragrant lips that feed the blood with flame !

The very earth seem'd bursting up, and heaven
Clung round and claspt us as in glowing arms,
To crush the wine of all your ripen'd beauty,
Which were a fitting sacrament for death—
Into a costly cup of life for me.

---

## SONG.

Ah ! 'tis like a tale of olden
  Time, long, long ago ;
When the world was in its golden
  Prime, and love was lord below !
Every vein of Earth was dancing
  With the Spring's new wine !
'Twas the pleasant time of flowers,
  When I met you, love of mine !
Ah ! some spirit sure was straying
  Out of heaven that day,
When I met you, Sweet ! a-Maying
  In the merry, merry May.

Little heart ! it shyly open'd
  Its red leaves' love-lore,
Like a rose that must be ripen'd
  To the dainty, dainty core.

But its beauties daily brighten,
  And it blooms so dear,—
Tho' a many Winters whiten,
  I go Maying all the year.
And my proud heart will be praying
  Blessings on the day,
When I met you, Sweet, a-Maying,
  In the merry, merry May.

---

## WEDDED LOVE.

The summer Night comes brooding down on Earth,
As Love comes brooding down on human hearts,
With bliss that hath no utterance save rich tears.
She floats in fragrance down the smiling dark,
Foldeth a kiss upon the lips of Life,—
Curtaineth into rest the weary world,—
And shuts us in with all our hid delights.
The Stars come sparkling thro' the gorgeous gloom,
Like dew-drops in the fields of heaven ; or tears
That hang rich jewels on the cheeks of Night.
A spirit-feel is in the solemn air.
The Flowers fold their cups like praying hands,
And with droopt heads await the blessing, Night
Gives with her silent magnanimity.

'Tis evening with the world ; but, in my soul
The light of wedded love is still at dawn !
And skies my world, an everlasting Dawn.
My heart rings out in music, like a lark
Hung in the charméd palace of the Morn,
That circles singing to its mate i' the nest,
With luminous being running o'er with song :
So my heart flutters round its mate at home !
There, with her eyes turned to her heart, she reads
The golden secrets written on its heaven,
And broodeth o'er its panting wealth of love,
As Night i' the hush and hallow of her beauty
Bares throbbing heaven to its most tremulous depths,
And broods in silence o'er her starry wealth.
And, fingering in her bosom's soft, white nest,
A fair babe, beautiful as Dawn in heaven,
Made of a Mother's richest thoughts of love,—
Lies like a smile of sunshine among lilies,
That giveth glory—drinketh fragrant life !
Sweet bud upon a Rose ! our plot of spring,
That bursts in bloom amid a wintry world !
How dear it is to mark th' immortal life
Deepen, and darken, in her large, round eyes,—
To watch Life's rose of dawn put forth its leaves,
And guess the perfumed secret of its heart—
And catch the silver words that come to break
The golden silence hung like heaven around.
But soft ! Elysium opens in my brain !

Dear Wife! with sweet, low voice, she syllables
Some precious music balm'd in her heart's book,
And I am flooded with melodious rain,
Like Nature standing crown'd with sunlit showers.

---

"As the surging heart o' the Sea hungers everlastingly
For the Moon, heaven-charméd by her influence:
As Star yearns to Star, with love palpitating like a dove,
Doth my heart yearn up to his bright eminence.

"O my Love, he seems to stand where Heaven leans so near at hand,
That from other worlds his lineaments take light:
And he fills my cup of wonder, and floods all my life with splendour,
As a glorious, golden Moon fills all the night.

"At his violet-sweet words my heart carols like a bird's,
And rich instincts burst from out it like heaven-flowers;
Wings bud in me at his kiss, and my being brims with bliss,
As a valley brims with life in spring-tide hours.

"O my life was dark and cold as the night-dews on the
world.
Waiting to be made alive with fire of dawn ;
Till his presence on me lighten'd and his blessing on me
brighten'd,
And my life like dews lit up for heaven shone."

---

Nay, Sweet Heart! that should be my song, who search
Love's lore in vain for meet similitudes
To symbol what thy love hath been to me.
The God lies prison'd in the mountain stone,
The muffled Music slumbers in the strings,
Awaiting the Deliverer's magic touch!
So, thou beloved! did I wait for Thee,
To waken at thy touch. My Tree of being
But made blind gropings in the dark, cold earth,
And moan'd and trembled, in the wintry air,
Stretching out naked hands to pluck at life :
Until you came, with all your light, and warmth,
Encircling round it like a summer heaven,
And fed, and clad it with your fragrant beauty,
Till budding branches burst on fire with bloom,
And into ripe fruits mellow'd goldenly.
My life lay barren as a desolate moor
That breaks, and burns, in twinkling green and gold,

When Spring doth greet it with her kiss of life.
As weary earth goes darkling thro' the night,
So my heart toil'd on, tearful with its burthen:
No beacon burn'd thro' all the gloom, to break
The surging sea of dark, with piers of light:
Then on a sudden rose the blessed Morn,
Sun-crown'd my life, made all things beautiful,
And gave the world its Eden-robes again.
My soul up-sprang full-statured, in the light,
Thy presence caught my heart up at the leap,
Wing'd like a young world from the hands of God!
Methought a thousand graves of buried hopes
Could crush it not from its proud eminence.
The Future's dim cloud-curtain rent in twain,
And lighten'd radiant revelation: All
Life's purpose dawn'd, as unto dying eyes
The dark of Death doth blossom into stars,
And since we met, thy life-long thought hath been
To be cup-bearer of the wine of joy
To one leal heart, and to make rich one life.
Pulse after pulse, thy life hath surged in mine,
Like sea-waves hurrying up the beach to crown
Their shore, and break in starry showers of light.
Thou hast brought radiant sunrise every morn,
Renewing all the glory past away.
Thy lavish love hath twined about my life,
Like the lush Wood-bine wedded to the Thorn;
Hiding its harshness with her wealth of flowers!

My heart drinks inspiration at thine eyes,
And lights my brain up as with fragrant flame:
Sweet eyes of starry tenderness, thro' which
The soul of some immortal sorrow looks!
Sorrow that addeth grace to loveliness,
As its sad bloom enricheth blushing fruit.
Dear Eyes! they have a radiant Alchemy,
And pierce my being with such quickening light
As makes my heart a jewel-mine of love;
Even as the Sun strikes thro' the dark cold Earth,
And fires her million veins with golden life.
My Life ran like a river in rocky ways,
And downward dasht, a sounding cataract!
But thine was like a quiet lake of beauty,
Soft-shadow'd round by gracious influences,
That gathers silently the wealth of earth,
And woos heaven till it melts down into it.
They mingled: and the glory, and the calm,
And royal-rich magnificence of thy love,
Closed round me, brooding into perfect rest,
And made my heart rejoice in all thy joy.
O blessings on thy true and tender heart!
How it hath gone forth like the Dove of old,
To bring some leaf of promise in Life's deluge!
Thou hast a strong up-soaring tendency,
That bears me god-ward, as the stalwart oak
Uplifts the clinging vine, and gives it growth.
Thy reverent heart familiarly doth take

Unconscious clasp of high and holy things,
Like little children playing of old with Christ;
And trusteth where it may not understand.
We have had sorrows, love! and wept the tears
That run the rose-hue from the cheeks of Life
But Grief hath jewels as Night hath her stars!
And she revealeth what we ne'er had known,
With Joy's wreath tumbled o'er our blinded eyes.
The heart is like an instrument whose strings
Steal magic music from Life's mystic frets;
The golden threads are spun thro' Suffering's fire,
Wherewith the marriage-robes for heaven are woven:
And all the rarest hues of human life
Take radiance, and are rainbow'd out in tears,
As water'd marble blooms a richer grain.
Thou'rt little changed, dear love! since first was wed
To mine, the blossom of thy crimson lips;
Thy beauty hath climaxt like a crescent Moon,
With glory great'ning to the golden full.
Thy flowers of spring are crown'd with summer fruits,
And thou hast put a queenlier presence on
With thy regality of Womanhood!
Yet Time but toucheth thee with mellowing shades
That set thy graces in a wealthier light.
Thy soul still looks with its rare smile of light,
From the Gate Beautiful of its palace-home,
Fair as the spirit of the evening Star
That lights its glory as a radiant porch

To beacon earth with a brief glimpse of heaven.
We are poor in this world's wealth, but rich in love;
And they who love feel rich in every thing.
The heart of Ocean—thick with gems, as earth
With blooms—is jewell'd like a Bride o' the East:
The heart of Heaven swarms with golden worlds—
A subtle heart of wealth hath our old world,
And darks of diamonds, grand as nights of stars:
But richer is the human heart that shrines
God's peerless wealth—the immortal jewel Love!
So let us live our life: and let our love,
Our large twin-love, bend o'er our little Babe,
As the calm grand old heavens bend over earth,
Revealing God's own starry thoughts and things!
So shall the image of our hearts' Ideal—
The angel nestling in her bud of life—
Smile upward in the mirror of her face
A daily beauty in our darkened ways,
And a perpetual feast of holy things.
O let us walk the world, so that our love
Burn like a blessed beacon, beautiful!
Upon the walls of Life's surrounding dark.
Ah! what a world 'twould be if love like ours
Made heaven in human hearts, and clothed with smiles
The sweet sad face of our Humanity!
What lives should quicken into sudden spring!
What flowers of glory burst their frozen soil!
Like the red pulse of Dawn thro' cold grey skies,

New life should flush up in the darken'd face
That readeth as a written epitaph
Above the grave of beauty and of soul!
Love-light should glimmer on the Helot's brow
As mellow moonlight silvers through a cloud,
And God should come into the mirkest being,
As Stars new-kindled splendour nights of space.

---

## THIS WORLD IS FULL OF BEAUTY.

THERE lives a voice within me, a guest-angel of my heart,
And its sweet lispings win me, till the tears a-trembling
start;
Up evermore it springeth, like some magic melody,
And evermore it singeth this sweet song of songs to me—
This world is full of beauty, as other worlds above;
And, if we did our duty, it might be full of love.

Night's starry tendernesses dower with glory evermore,
Morn's budding, bright, melodious hour comes sweetly as
of yore;
But there be million hearts accurst, where no sweet sun-
bursts shine,
And there be million hearts athirst for Love's immortal
wine.

This world is full of beauty, as other worlds above;
And, if we did our duty, it might be full of love.

If faith, and hope, and kindness pass'd, as coin, 'twixt heart and heart;
How, thro' the eye's tear-blindness, should the sudden soul upstart!
The dreary, dim, and desolate, should wear a sunny bloom,
And Love should spring from buried Hate, like flowers o'er Winter's tomb.
This world is full of beauty, as other worlds above;
And, if we did our duty, it might be full of love.

With truth our uttered language, Angels might talk with men,
And God-illumined earth should see the golden Age again:
The burthen'd heart should soar in mirth like Morn's young prophet-lark,
And Misery's last tear wept on earth, quench Hell's last cunning spark.
For this world is full of beauty, as other worlds above;
And, if we did our duty, it might be full of love.

Lo! plenty ripens round us, yet awakes the cry for bread,
The millions still are toiling, crusht, and clad in rags, unfed!

While sunny hills and valleys richly blush with fruit and
grain,
But the paupers in the palace rob their toiling fellow-
men.
This world is full of beauty, as other worlds above ;
And, if we did our duty, it might be full of love.

Dear God ! what hosts are trampled 'mid this killing
crush for gold !
What noble hearts are sapp'd of love ! what spirits lose
life's hold !
Yet a merry world it might be, opulent for all, and aye,
With its lands that ask for labour, and its wealth that
wastes away.
This world is full of beauty, as other worlds above ;
And, if we did our duty, it might be full of love.

The leaf-tongues of the forest, and the flow'r-lips of the
sod—
The happy Birds that hymn their raptures in the ear of
God—
The summer wind that bringeth music over land and sea,
Have each a voice that singeth this sweet song of songs
to me—
This world is full of beauty, as other worlds above ;
And, if we did our duty, it might be full of love.

## TO A BELOVED ONE.

HEAVEN hath its crown of Stars, the Earth
Her glory-robe of flowers—
The Sea its gems—the grand old Woods
Their songs and greening showers:
The Birds have homes, where leaves and blooms
In beauty wreathe above;
High yearning hearts, their rainbow-dream—
And we, Sweet! we have love.

We walk not with the jewell'd Great,
Where Love's dear name is sold;
Yet have we wealth we would not give
For all their world of gold!
We revel not in Corn and Wine,
Yet have we from above
Manna divine, and we'll not pine:
Do we not live and love?

There's sorrow for the toiling poor,
On Misery's bosom nurst;
Rich robes for ragged souls, and Crowns
For branded brows Cain-curst!
But Cherubim, with clasping wings,
Ever about us be,
And, happiest of God's happy things!
There's love for you and me.

Thy lips, that kiss till death, have turn'd
Life's water into wine ;
The sweet life melting thro' thy looks,
Hath made my life divine.
All Love's dear promise hath been kept,
Since thou to me wert given ;
A ladder for my soul to climb,
And summer high in heaven,

I know, dear heart ! that in our lot
May mingle tears and sorrow ;
But, Love's rich Rainbow's built from tears
To-day, with smiles To-morrow.
The sunshine from our sky may die,
The greenness from Life's tree,
But ever, 'mid the warring storm,
Thy nest shall shelter'd be.

I see thee ! Ararat of my life,
Smiling the waves above !
Thou hail'st me Victor in the strife,
And beacon'st me with love,
The world may never know, dear heart !
What I have found in thee ;
But, tho' nought to the world, dear heart !
Thou'rt all the world to me.

# HOOD.

## WHO SANG THE SONG OF THE SHIRT.

'Tis the old story !—ever the blind world
Knows not its Angels of Deliverance
Till they stand glorified 'twixt earth and heaven.
It stones the martyr : then, with praying hands,
Sees the God mount his chariot of fire,
And calls sweet names, and worships what it spurn'd.
It slays the Man to deify the Christ :
And then how lovingly 'twill bind the brows
Where late its thorn-crown laught with bloody lips—
Red, and rejoicing from grim Murder's kiss !
To those who walk beside them, great men seem
Mere common earth ; but distance makes them stars.
As dying limbs do lengthen out in death,
So grows the stature of their after-fame ;
And then we gather up their glorious words,
And treasure up their names with loving care.
So Hood, our Poet, lived his martyr-life :
With a swift soul that travell'd at rare speed,
And struck such flashes from its flinty road,
That by its trail of radiance through the dark,
We almost feature th' unknown Future's face—
And went uncrown'd to his untimely tomb.
Certes, the World did praise his glorious Wit—
The merry Jester with his cap and bells !

And sooth, his wit was like Ithuriel's spear;
But 'twas mere lightning from the cloud of his life,
Which held at heart most rich and blessed rain
Of tears melodious, that are worlds of love;
And Rainbows, that would bridge from earth to heaven,
And Light, that would have shone like Joshua's sun
Above our long death-grapple with the Wrong;
And thunder-voices, with their Words of fire,
To melt the Slave's chain, and the Tyrant's crown.
His wit?—a kind smile just to hearten us!—
Rich foam-wreaths on the waves of lavish life,
That flasht o'er precious pearls and golden sands.
But, there was that beneath surpassing show!
The starry soul that shines when all is dark!—
Endurance, that can suffer and grow strong—
Walk through the world with bleeding feet, and smile!—
Love's inner light, that kindles Life's rare colours!
And thoughts that swathe Humanity with such glory
As limns the outline of the coming God;
And wine of Beauty for the panting soul.
In him were gleams of such heroic splendours
As light this cold, dark world up as a star
Array'd in glory for the eyes of heaven:
And a great heart that beat according music
With theirs of old—God-likest, royallest men!
A conquering heart! which Circumstance, that frights
The Many down from Love's transfiguring height,
Aye mettled into martial attitude.

He might have clutcht the palm of Victory
In the world's wrestling ring of mightiest deeds ;
But he went down like a rich Argosy
At sea, just glimmering into sight of home,
With its rare freightage from diviner climes.
The world may never know the wealth it lost,
When Hood went darkling to his tearful tomb,
So mighty in his undevelopt force !
With all his crowding unaccomplished hopes !
Th' unuttered wealth and glory of his soul !
And all the music ringing round his life,
And poems stirring in his dying brain !
O ! blessings on him for the songs he sang—
Which yearned about the world till then for birth !
How like a bonny bird of God he came,
And pour'd his heart in music for the Poor ;
Who sit in gloom while sunshine floods the land,
And feel, through darkness, for the hand of Help !
And trampled Manhood heard, and claimed his crown
And trampled Womanhood sprang up ennobled !
The human soul lookt radiantly through rags !
And there was melting of cold hearts, as when
The ripening sunlight fingers frozen flowers.
O ! blessings on him for the songs he sang !
When all the stars of happy thought had set
In many a mind, his spirit walkt the gloom
Clothed on with beauty, as the regal Moon
Walks her night-kingdom, turning clouds to light.

Our Champion ! with his heart too big to beat
In bonds,—our Poet in his pride of power !
Ay, we'll remember him who fought our fight,
And chose the Martyr's robe of flame, and spurn'd
The gold and purple of the glistering slave.
His Mausoleum is the People's heart,
There he lies crown'd and glorified,—our King
In state, with singing robe wrapt richly round.
But 'tis not meet, my England, his dear dust
Should lie where splendid flatteries flaunt on tombs,
As treachery serves to brighten wanton tears—
With not a line of letter'd love to tell
What mighty heart lies quencht and broken there.
So let us build our Poet's monument !
With passionate hearts of love for corner-stones,
And tears that temper for immortal fame.
And it were well, my England, shouldst thou come
To weep some honest drops above his grave.
Our Hood is worthier of eternal praise
And blessings, and dear heart-immunities,
Than warrior Wellington, who rode to fame
On Death's white horse by Battle's crimson path.

## THE SINGER.

UP out of the Corn the Lark caroll'd in light,
Like a new splendour sprung from the dark husk of Night,
Green light shimmer'd laughing o'er forest and sod ;
The rich sky was full of the presence of God,
As with brave careless rapture he lavisht around
Rare violet fancies and rose-leaves of sound :
All thro' the Morn's sun-city sea-like his psalm
With melodious waves dasht the bright world of calm :
BUT HEAVILY HUNG THE DROOPT EARS OF THE CORN :
THEY WERE GATHERING GOLD IN THE DEWY MORN.

And he sang, as on heaven's fire-grains he had fed,
Till his heart's merry wine had made drunken his head.
How he sang ! as his honey in Life's cells ne'er dwindled,
And beale-fires of Joy on all Life's hills were kindled :
O ! he sang, as he felt that to singing was given
The magic to build rainbow-stairways to heaven !
And he could not have sung with more lusty cheer,
Had all the world listened a-tiptoe to hear !
ALL THE WHILE HEAVILY HUNG THE CORN,
AND ITS DROWSY EARS HEARD NOT THE SWEETHEART OF MORN.

## ICHABOD.

Seven Summers' Suns have set ! and earth is once more
sweetly flooded
With fragrance, for the virgin-leaves and violet-banks have
budded :
Heaven claspeth Earth, as round the heart first broodeth
Love's rich glow ;
A blush of Flowers is mantling where the lush green
grasses grow !
All things feel summering sunward, golden tides flood
down the air,
Which burns, as Angel-visitants had left a glory there !
But darkness on my aching spirit shrouds the merry
shine,—
I long to feel a gush of Spring in this poor heart of mine.

Morn opes Heaven's opal portal, back the golden gates
are drawn,
And all the fields of glory blossom with the crimson Dawn:
But never comes thy clasping hand, or carol of thy lips,
That made my heart sing like a God, when bursting
Death's eclipse.
Sweet voice ! it came like saintly music, quiring angels
make,
When pain sat heavy on my brow, and heart was like to
break :

Methought such love gave wings to climb some starry
thorne to win ;
Thou didst so lift my life's horizon—letting heaven in.

I'm thinking, darling, of the days when life was all divine,
And love was aye the silver chord that bound my heart
to thine ;
When life bloom'd at thy coming, as the green earth greets
the sun,
And, like two dew-drops in a kiss, our twin souls wed in
one.
Ah ! still I feel ye at my heart ! and, 'mid the stir and
strife,
Ye sometimes lead my feet to walk the angel-side of Life !
The magic music yearns within, as unto thee I turn,
And those brave eyes, a-blaze with soul, thro' all my
being burn.

Come back,—come back ; I long to clasp thee in these
arms, mine own !
Lavish my heart upon thy lips, and make my love the
Crown
And Arc of Triumph to thy life. Why tarry ? Time
hath cast
Strange shadows on my spirit since we met and mingled
last !

Yet there be joys to crown thee with, the sunshine and
the sweet
Are hived, like honey, in my heart, to share them when
we meet :
How I have hoarded up my life ! how tenderly I strove
To make my heart fit home for thee, its nestling Bird of
love !

God bless thee ! once the radiant world thy beauty crown-
like wore,
But life hath lost a tender grace that cometh never more !
The flowers will bud again in spring, and happy birds make
love,
With melting hearts, a-brooding o'er their passion in the
grove.
But thou wilt never more come back, to clothe my heart
with Spring :
Dear God ! Love's sweetest chord is turn'd to Pain's
most jarring string !
The Glory hath departed ! and my spirit pants to go
Where 'mid Life's troubled waters, 'twill not see the
wreck below.

## NOT LOST, BUT GONE BEFORE.

One of God's own Darlings was my bosom's nestling Dove,
With her looks of love and sunshine, and her voice so rich and low:
How it trembled thro' my life, like an Immortal's kiss of love!
How its music yearns thro' all my memory now!

O! her beauty rainbows round me, and her sweet smile, silverly
As a song, fills all the silence of the Midnight's charmèd hours:
And I know from out her grave she'll send her love in death to me,
By the Spring, in smiling utterance of Flowers.

O! my Love, too good for Earth, has gone into the world of light;
It was hard, she said, to leave me, but the Lord had need of her;
And she walks the heaven in glory, like a Star i' the crown of Night,
With the Beautiful and Blessed mingling there.

Gone before me, to be clothéd on with bridal robe of
white,
Where Love's blossom flowers to fruit of knowledge,—
Suffering's glorified !
And my love shall make me meet and worthy of her presence bright,
That in heaven I may claim her as my Bride.

---

## THE CHIVALRY OF LABOUR.

UPROUSE ye now, brave brother-band,
With honest heart, and working hand ;
We are but few, toil-tried, and true,
Yet hearts beat high to dare and do ;
And who would not a champion be
In Labour's lordlier Chivalry ?
We fight ! but bear no bloody brand,
We fight to free our Fatherland :
We fight that smiles of love may glow
On lips where curses quiver now !
Hurrah ! hurrah ! true Knights are we
In Labour's lordlier Chivalry.

O ! there be hearts that ache to see
The day-dawn of our victory;

Eyes full of heart-break with us plead,
And Watchers weep and Martyrs bleed:
O! who would not a Champion be
In Labour's lordlier Chivalry?

Work, Brothers mine; work, hand and brain;
We'll win the Golden Age again:
And Love's Millennial morn shall rise
In happy hearts, and blessed eyes.
Hurrah! hurrah! true Knights are we
In Labour's lordlier Chivalry.

---

## THE CHIVALRY OF LABOUR EXHORTED TO THE WORSHIP OF BEAUTY.

Our world oft turns in gloom, and Life hath many a perilous way,
Yet there's no path so desolate and thorny, cold and gray,
But Beauty like a Beacon burns above the dark of strife,
And like an Alchemist aye turns all things to golden life.
On human hearts her presence droppeth precious manna down,
On human brows her glory gathers like a coming crown:

Her smile lights up Life's troubled stream, and Love, the
swimmer ! lives ;
And O 'tis brave to battle for the guerdon that she gives!
Then let us worship Beauty with the knightly faith of old,
O Chivalry of Labour toiling for the Age of Gold !

The first-fruits of the Past at Beauty's shrine are offer'd up,
From which a vintage meet for Gods she crusheth in her
cup :
And from the living Present doth she press the rare new
wine,
To glad the hearts of all her lovers with a draught divine.
Earth's crowning miracle ! she comes ! with blessing lips,
that part
Like mid-May's rose flusht open with the fragrance of her
heart :
And life turns to her colour—kindles with her light—like
flowers
That garner up the golden fire, and suck the mellow
showers.
Come let us worship Beauty with the knightly faith of old,
O Chivalry of Labour toiling for the Age of Gold !

Come let us worship Beauty where the budding Spring
doth flower,
And lush green leaves and grasses flush out sweeter every
hour ;

Or Summer's tide of splendour floods the lap o' the World
once more,
With riches like a sea that surges jewels on its shore.
Come feel her ripening influence when Morning feasts our
eyes—
Thro' open gates of glory—with a glimpse of Paradise :
Or queenly Night sits crowned, smiling down the purple
gloom,
And Stars, like Heaven's fruitage, melt i' the glory of their
bloom.
Come let us worship Beauty with the knightly faith of old,
O Chivalry of Labour toiling for the Age of Gold!

Come from the den of darkness and the city's soil of sin,
Put on your radiant Manhood, and the Angel's blessing win!
Where wealthier sunlight comes from Heaven, like wel-
come-smiles of God,
And Earth's blind yearnings leap to life in flowers, from
out the sod :
Come worship Beauty in the forest-temple, dim and hush,
Where stands Magnificence dreaming! and God burneth
in the bush :
Or where the old hills worship with their silence for a
psalm,
Or ocean's weary heart doth keep the sabbath of its calm.
Come let us worship Beauty with the knightly faith of old,
O Chivalry of Labour toiling for the Age of Gold!

Come let us worship Beauty: she hath subtle power to start
Heroic word and deed out-flashing from the humblest heart:
Great feelings will gush unawares, and freshly as the first
Rich Rainbow that up startled Heaven in tearful splendour
burst.
O blessed are her lineaments, and wondrous are her ways
To repicture God's worn likeness in the suffering human
face!
Our bliss shall richly overbrim like sunset in the west,
And we shall dream immortal dreams and banquet with
the Blest.
Then let us worship Beauty with the knightly faith of old,
O Chivalry of Labour toiling for the Age of Gold!

---

## WHEN I COME HOME.

Around me Life's hell of fierce Ardours burns,
When I come home, when I come home;
Over me Heaven with her starry heart yearns,
When I come home, when I come home.
For the feast of Gods garnisht, the palace of Night
At a thousand star-windows is throbbing with light.
London makes mirth! but I know God hears
The sobs i' the dark, and the dropping of tears;

For I feel that he listens down Night's great dome—
When I come home, when I come home,
    Home, home, when I come home,
    Far i' the night when I come home.

I walk under Night's triumphal arch,
    When I come home, when I come home,
Exulting with life like a Conqueror's march,
    When I come home, when I come home.
I pass by the rich-chamber'd mansions that shine,
Overflowing with splendour like goblets with wine:
I have fought, I have vanquisht, the dragon of Toil,
And before me my golden Hesperides smile!
And O but Love's flowers make rich the gloom,
When I come home, when I come home!
    Home, home, when I come home,
    Far i' the night when I come home.

O the sweet, merry mouths up-turn'd to be kist,
    When I come home, when I come home!
How the younglings yearn from the hungry nest,
    When I come home, when I come home!
My weary worn heart into sweetness is stirr'd,
And it dances and sings like a singing Bird,
On the branch nighest heaven,—a-top of my life:
As I clasp thee, my winsome, wooing Wife!

And thy pale cheek with rich, tender passion doth bloom
When I come home, when I come home,
 Home, home, when I come home,
 Far i' the night when I come home.

Clouds furl off the shining face of my life,
 When I come home, when I come home,
And leave heaven bare on thy bosom, sweet Wife!
 When I come home, when I come home.
With her smiling Energies,—Faith warm and bright,—
With Love glory-crown'd and serenely alight—
With her womanly beauty and queenly calm,
She steals to my heart with her blessing of balm;
And O but the wine of love sparkles with foam,
When I come home, when I come home!
 Home, home, when I come home!
 Far i' the night when I come home.

---

## THE THREE SPIRITS.

They were three Spirits fresh from God's own hand,
And beautifuller ne'er took mortal mould,
They had worn vestures of the undefiled,
At spirit-spousals sang the nuptial song,
Sat down with Gods and Heroes, held high converse

With Milton and the mighty men of old,
Divine old Socrates and deathless sages,
The martyr'd Prophets and the warrior-saints,
Who fought as we do now, and wrestled down
Doubt's grim despairs, with pangs and quenchless faith.
Glory tiara'd their immortal brows,
Their lips were yet alive with seraph-fire,
And locks bedropt rich dews of Paradise :
They lookt a fore-taste and fore-feel of heaven
Christ-like they came to wear old Earth's life-harness,
And yoke their fiery sun-steeds in her furrows.
They came to battle, toil in tears, and pray,
" Our Father," with the family of Men.
'Twas midnight in the husht and moonlit land,
The heavens had on their silver robe of stars,
And earth had on her silver robe of dew,
When they first lookt like smiles of God, through eyes
Where struggling heaven-light shone half-drown'd in tears,
As rainy sunbeams strike a watery world.
They grew sweet babes, where fond hearts set Love's
throne,
Heaven breathed about them, Angels sang to them,
And joy was with them in their innocence.
Their dawn of being broaden'd into day,
And they had sprung to Manhood unawares.
The lusty blood ran brave fire in their veins,
Life's surging waves, with them, were at mad-plunge,
And plough'd the passionate heart with tempest-beat.

Then high thoughts burst like battle on their souls,
Rousing and stern as in the noon of night
The clarion's clangour smites a sleeping host!
And gorgeous Visions, glory-clad, swept by.
Sinew and thew were strung to win at least
The table-land that girds the mount of Fame.
And one went down to moil in Mammon's mine,
For love of Gold; thenceforth in his warpt heart,
The Devil at death-grips set himself to God,
And day by day worm'd out some trace divine!
Day unto day, Gold rotted out the soul.
Still he toil'd on for Gold, sweet! damning Gold!
The poor man's sweat, and tears, and blood, congeal'd;
And he waxt wealthy! all around him rose
The hoarded heaps, like trophies after battle,
Or tribute-treasure flung at Monarchs' feet.
He turn'd to what he fed on, dust to dust;
The angel-plumes once moulted, grew no more!
The God dwarft in him, and his heart was hoary
Before Time's silver mark had blancht his brow.
And one up-reared a fame which stood apart
In the world's gaze, as 'mid old Tadmor's ruins
Some column loometh in the eye of sunset.
He crown'd with a beacon-fire the reef which wreckt
The mighty of all time. His marvellous name
Moved men's tongues regally as Euroclydon,
The storm-wind! wakes the voices of old ocean.
Leviathan of blood! what crimson seas

He spilt to revel in ; his path to empire
Was wasted hearts and desolated lands.
The other trode the world's face poor as Christ,
Drank gall and wormwood ; lived Gethsemane,
In many a midnight solitude of heart !
Loved, hoped, and nurst large faith in human-kind,
Wept glorious tears that telescope the soul,
And bring heaven nearer to the eyes of Faith !
The hounds of hell bay'd at him, hoary Evil
Breathed blighting influence on his heart,
To turn it to a Upas-tree, and kill
All nestling birds of love. With tears and travail
He walkt the furnace, trode Earth's stony ways,
And beat his rugged path with bleeding feet.
Yet nought bore down his heart, or blencht his faith,
And many a cloud-rift radiantly rent,
Dropt blessing dear as parted lips of love.
From suffering he won strength to throw the world ;
And when the fight ran sorest, his roused spirit
Went forth a Conquerer ! wrapt in robes of victory.
Amid the mirk and mire, he kept his heart
A temple for the Beautiful ! all warm
And bright, with blessed light of Love, that window
Of our dim life, which ever opes on God !
He trimmed Love's lamp in poor men's hearts and homes,
And in the world's waste places his life blossom'd.
So each built up a life. Time's scaffolding
Fell from them, and they stood in God's eye bare !

Into the silent land, they pass'd the Grave,
Which Spring had made a beautiful gate of flowers ;
On wings of wonder won the starry threshold
Of God, where like to like is gauged and garnered.
They stood where Paradise uprear'd its portals,
And shook down splendours, palpitated bliss—
Like a town full of triumph—heart of love.
O in that hour how shook the rich man's soul !
He stood there beggar'd, poorest of the poor !
Gold would not purchase heaven ; and if it might,
Eternity ran 'twixt him and his riches :
And he went wailing with his world of woe.
The other had gambled for a life, and lost,
Let slip his chance for an eternity !
For fame, had barter'd an immortal birthright ;
For name on Earth had sold Heaven's heritage ;
And there the gates of glory on him closed.
The poor man came, and his meek tearful eyes
Grew luminous, as lit with sudden sun.
Divinity leapt up full-statured, when
His life burst its worn manacle of clay,
And wore God's splendour round it like a raiment.
Throbbing with glory like a midnight star,
All heaven was husht to hear the Lord's "Well done."
Then shining hosts and quiring orbs sang "Welcome,"
And angels crown'd him in their Capitol.
For in his heart he kept God's image bright.
Love was his life-blood. Thro' the long work-d· y—

The dark and terrible night-time—aye, to death,
He nurst his love : and God himself is love.
And there be none of all the poorest poor
That walk the world, worn heart-bare, none so poor
But they may bring a little human love
To mend the world. And God himself is love.

---

## TO-DAY AND TO-MORROW.

High hopes that burn'd like stars sublime,
  Go down i' the Heavens of Freedom ;
And true hearts perish in the time
  We bitterliest need 'em !
But never sit we down and say
  There's nothing left but sorrow :
We walk the Wilderness To-day,
  The Promised Land To-morrow.

Our birds of song are silent now,
  There are no flowers blooming ;
Yet life beats in the frozen bough,
  And Freedom's Spring is coming !
And Freedom's tide comes up alway,
  Tho' we may stand in sorrow :
And our good Bark, a-ground To-day,
  Shall float again To-morrow.

Thro' all the long, dark night of years
  The People's cry ascendeth,
And Earth is wet with blood and tears:
  But our meek sufferance endeth!
The Few shall not for ever sway,
  The Many moil in sorrow:
The Powers of Hell are strong To-day,
  But Christ shall rise To-morrow.

Tho' hearts brood o'er the Past, our eyes
  With smiling Futures glisten!
For, lo! our day bursts up the skies:
  Lean out your souls and listen!
The world rolls Freedom's radiant way,
  And ripens with her sorrow:
Keep heart! who bear the Cross To-day,
  Shall wear the Crown To-morrow.

O Youth! flame-earnest, still aspire,
  With energies immortal!
To many a heaven of Desire,
  Our yearning opes a portal!
And tho' Age wearies by the way,
  And hearts break in the furrow,
We'll sow the golden grain To-day,—
  The Harvest comes To-morrow.

Build up heroic lives, and all
  Be like a sheathen sabre,
Ready to flash out at God's call,
  O Chivalry of Labour !
Triumph and Toil are twins : and aye
  Joy suns the cloud of Sorrow ;
And 'tis the martyrdom To-day,
  Brings victory To-morrow.

---

## HUSBAND AND WIFE.

O PROUDLY I stood in the rare Sunrise,
  As the dawn of your beauty brake ;
But I fear'd for the storm, as I lookt at the skies,
  And trembled for your sweet sake !
And O, may the evil days come not, I said,
  As I yearn'd o'er my tender blossom !
Strong arm of love ! shelter the dear one's head :
  And I nestled you in my bosom.
May the tears never dim the love-light of her eye,—
  May her Life be all Spring-weather !—
Was the prayer of my heart, ere you, Love, and I,
  Were Husband and Wife together.

But the suns will shine, and the rains will fall,
  On the loftiest, lowliest spot!
And there's mourning and merriment mingled for all
  That inherit the human lot.
So we've suffer'd and sorrow'd and grown more strong,
  Heart-to-heart, side-by-side, we have striven,
With the love that makes summer-tide all the year long,
  And the heart that is its own heaven!
We clung the more close as the storm swept by,
  And kept the nest warm in cold weather:
And seldom we've falter'd since you, Love, and I,
  Have been Husband and Wife together!

Like the sweet wild flowers of the wilderness,
  You have dwelt life to life with Nature;
And caught the wild beauty and grace of her ways,
  And grown to her heavenlier stature!
In golden calm, and in quickening strife,
  Hath your womanly worth unfolden:
And sunshine and show'r have enricht your life,
  And ripen'd its harvest golden.
There is good in the grimmest cloud o' the sky,
  There are blessings in wintry weather:
Even Grief hath its glory, since you, Love, and I,
  Have been Husband and Wife together.

O, Life is not perfect with Love's first kiss:
  Who would win the blessing must wrestle;

And the deeper the sorrow, the dearer the bliss,
  That in its rich core may nestle !
Our Angels oft greet us in tearful guise,
  And our saviours come in sorrow :
While the murkiest midnight that frowns from the skies.
  Is at heart a radiant Morrow !
We laugh and we cry, we sing and we sigh,
  And life will have wintry weather !
So we'll hope, and love on, since you, Love, and I,
  Are Husband and Wife together.

---

## NO JEWELLED BEAUTY IS MY LOVE.

No jewelled Beauty is my Love,
  Yet in her earnest face
There's such a world of tenderness,
  She needs no other grace.
Her smiles, and voice, around my life
  In light and music twine,
And dear, O very dear to me.
  Is this sweet Love of mine.

O joy ! to know there's one fond heart,
  Beats ever true to me :
It sets mine leaping like a lyre,
  In sweetest melody :

My soul up-springs, a Deity !
  To hear her voice divine,
And dear, O very dear to me,
  Is this sweet Love of mine.

If ever I have sigh'd for wealth,
  'Twas all for her, I trow ;
And if I win Fame's victor-wrath,
  I'll twine it on her brow.
There may be forms more beautiful,
  And souls of sunnier shine,
But none, O none, so dear to me,
  As this sweet Love of mine.

---

## THE KINGLIEST KINGS

Ho ! ye who in a noble work
  Win scorn, as flames draw air,
And in the way where Lions lurk,
  God's image bravely bear ;
Tho' trouble-tried, and torture-torn,
The kingliest Kings are crown'd with thorn.

Life's glory, like the bow in heaven,
  Still springeth from the cloud ;
And soul ne'er soar'd the starry Seven,
  But Pain's fire-chariot rode.

They've battled best who've boldliest borne,
The kingliest Kings are crown'd with thorn.

The Martyr's fire-crown on the brow
Doth into glory burn :
And tears that from Love's torn heart flow,
To pearls of spirit turn.
Our dearest hopes in pangs are born,
The kingliest Kings are crown'd with thorn.

As beauty in Death's cerement shrouds,
And Stars bejewel Night,
God-splendours live in dim heart-clouds,
And suffering worketh might,
The mirkiest hour is mother o' Morn,
The kingliest Kings are crown'd with thorn.

## MARTYRS FOR HUNGARY AND ROME.
### 1850.

THEY are gone!
When on earthquake-edge they slumbered,
Who have man accurst;
And Hope's blossoms, many-numbered,
Into flower burst;
When our hearts, like throbbing drums,
Beat for Freedom; sang, She comes!
God! they stumbled among tombs.

They are gone!
Freedom's strong ones, young and hoary,
Beautiful in faith!
And her first dawn-blush of glory
Gilds their camp of death!
There they lie in shrouds of blood;
Murder'd where for Right they stood—
Murder'd, Christ-like, doing good.

They are gone!
And 'tis good to die up-giving
Valour's vengeful breath,
To make Heroes of the living,—
Thus divine is death.

One by one, dear hearts! they've left us,
Yet Hope hath not all bereft us:
Still we man the breach they cleft us.

They are here!
Here, where life ran ruddy rain,
When power from God seem'd wrencht:
Here, where tears fall—molten brain!
And hands are agony-clencht!
Look, Love lifts the veil; ah! now
There's glory, where the glow
Of Pain's fire-crown seam'd each brow.

They are here!
In the Etna of each heart,
Where Vengeance laughs hell-mirth,
In the silent tears that start
O'er their glorious worth!
Tears? ay, tears of fire, proud Weepers!
For these soul-sepultured sleepers:
Fire! to smite Death's blood-seed reapers.

They are here!
With us in the march of time,
Beating at our side!
Let us live their lives sublime,
Die as they have died!

Wait : these Martyrs yet shall come,
Myriad-fold, from their heart-tomb !
In the Tyrant's day of doom.

---

## LOVE ME.

"All dear as the feeling when first-flowers start,
Thou cam'st in thy musical lightness :
And the cloud wept itself in rich rain on my heart,
That had hidden thy beauty and brightness.
'Twas as Life's topmost window oped suddenly, bright
With the glittering face of an Angel,
The sweet secret out-flasht on thy forehead of light,
And I knew thee, my own love-Evangel !
O how shall I crown thee, Love, on my heart's throne,
Thou art so far, far above me ?"
And aye as her dear eyes lookt love in mine own,
The Maiden answered, "Love me."

"My Beloved is fair as some beautiful star
That walks in an air of glory :
And her large-hearted looks and her lineaments are
As some Queen's of the old Greek story !

There's never night now, since those dear eyes of thine
Smiled on me their soft sweet splendour,
And I drank of the wine of thy kisses divine :
O what for such love shall I render ?"
And aye, as I knelt at my true Love's shrine,
She bent in her beauty above me :
And aye, as her sweet eyes lookt love into mine,
The Maiden answered, "Love me."

"O could my heart, mountain-region'd in bliss,
Thy life with Love's affluence dower,
Thou should'st have heaven in a world e'en like this,
And the joy of a life in each hour !
Thou should'st go forth like a conquering queen,
Reaping rich heartfuls of treasure,
Nor strive where the worn of heart wearily glean
But handfuls, in harvesting pleasure."
And aye, as I knelt at my true Love's shrine,
She bent in her beauty above me :
And aye, as her sweet eyes lookt love into mine,
The Maiden answered, "Love me."

## LOVE'S FAIRY RING.

While Titans war with social Jove,
 My own sweet wife and I
We make Elysium in our love,
 And let the world go by!
O never hearts beat half so light
 With crownéd Queen or King!
O never world was half so bright
 As is our fairy-ring,
 Dear love!
 Our hallowed fairy-ring.

Our world of empire is not large,
 But priceless wealth it holds;
A little heaven links marge to marge,
 But what rich realms it folds!
And clasping all from outer strife
 Sits Love with folden wing,
A-brood o'er dearer life-in-life,
 Within our fairy-ring,
 Dear love!
 Our hallowed fairy-ring.

Thou leanest thy true heart on mine,
 And bravely bearest up!
Aye mingling Love's most precious wine
 In Life's most bitter cup!

And evermore the circling hours
    New gifts of glory bring ;
We live and love like happy flowers,
    All in our fairy-ring,
                Dear love !
    Our hallowed fairy-ring.

We've known a many sorrows, Sweet !
    We've wept a many tears,
And often trod with trembling feet
    Our pilgrimage of years.
But when our sky grew dark and wild,
    All closelier did we cling :
Clouds broke to beauty as you smiled,
    Peace crown'd our fairy-ring,
                Dear love !
    Our hallowed fairy-ring.

Away, grim Lords of Murderdom ;
    Away, O Hate, and Strife !
Hence, revellers, reeling drunken from
    Your feast of human life !
Heaven shield our little Goshen round,
    From ills that with them spring,
And never be their footprints found
    Within our fairy-ring,
                Dear love !
    Our hallowed fairy-ring.

But, come ye who the Truth dare own,
Or work in Love's dear name ;
Come all who wear the Martyr's crown—
The Mystic's robe of flame !
Sweet souls, a Christless world doth doom
Like birds smote blind to sing—
For such, we'll aye make welcome room
Within our fairy-ring,
Dear love !
Our hallowed fairy-ring.

---

## NEW YEAR'S EVE IN EXILE.

Warriors of Freedom who for heritage
Wear on their brows a mark as curst as Cain's,
The flower and chivalry of many lands
Betrothed to Martyrdom as to a Bride,—
Had met together, a strange companie !
But brothers, battling in one sacred cause.
They were heroic souls who had lain life's all
On Freedom's hungry Altar, and gone forth
Clad in the spirit of self-sacrifice,
To roam a thankless world with homeless hearts,—
Men who had tost on Danger's wildest waves,
For whom a radiant Victory ever shone :

Like Hero on her watch-tower with her torch,
Lighting her lover through the shadow of death,—
Men who had broken Battle's burning lines,
Dealing life with their looks, death with their hands,
And strode like Salamanders through War's flame ;
And in the last stern charge of desperate valour,
On Death's scythe dasht with force that turn'd its edge.
Some were but youths, yet with such manhood flusht,
By eager leaps to catch at lordlier life,
They had attained the old heroic stature.
Some had grown grey with battle, some with years,
And there were ancient Sorrows grand as kings,
Of an old peerless line. Such silent Griefs
And Sufferings crown'd for immortality.
Earnest as fire they sate, and reverent
As though a God were present in their midst ;
Stern, but serene and hopeful, prayerful, brave,
As Cromwell's Ironsides on an eve of battle ;
Each individual life as clencht and knit,
As though beneath their robes their fingers clutcht
The weapon sworn to strike a Tyrant down.
Such proud Belief did lift their kindling brows,
Such glowing purpose hunger'd in their eyes,
With fire enough to set a world in flames.
No servile souls, that at your fixéd look,
Like meek worms, writhe into their darkening holes.
And One up-rose to word the Thought than run
Hot to their hearts and glittering to their brows ;

An old man, with the mournfull'st, thin, grey hair;
The lines of suffering in his face seem'd drawn
Tight with the mortal tug of Agony;
But with sad majesty he smiled, and splendour
Broke sweetly from the furrows of his face,
As wrinkles on the waters laugh with light.
Dilating as a Prophet's wings of flame
Flutter'd within him—all his aspect burn'd
With an unearthly fire. He was caught up
The mount Transfiguration, with eyes fixt
On air, as though he talkt with one beyond.
He stood there looking down the unseen time,
Like some hoar Hill that lifts its solemn peak
To catch the unrisen Morn, while all the plains
Are drowsed and darkling. He already sunn'd
Him in the glory of the coimng Day;
And his words swept their yielding, springing hearts,
As strong winds take a field of billowing corn.
"The merry Bells are jubilant To-night
Through all the land of Exile; blithe wine laughs
Its bubbling laughter,—winking gem-like eyes,
And leaps up in the beaker like red lips
Whose kisses storm the inner gates of bliss.
But not with mirth, and song, and dainty feast,
We meet to hold our solemn festival.
We wait the wine of Freedom; when it runs
We shall wax merry, too,—perchance grow drunken—
They keep it ripening to such mellow age!

And we shall banquet like Immortals fed
By Hebe's hand at the Ambrosial feasts.
The New Year flashes on us sadly grand,
Leaps in our midst with ringing armour on,
Strikes a mail'd hand in ours, and bids us arm
Ere the first trumpet sound the hour of onset.
Dense darkness lies on Europe's winter-world.
Stealthy and grim the Bear comes creeping on,
Out of the North, and all the Peoples sleep
By Freedom's smouldering watch-fire : there is none
To snatch the brand, and dash it in his face.
Old England sleeps, and still the Bear creeps on.
Ah ! she forgetteth how, in the old years,
The great hearts of her glorious Commonwealth
Sent thunder-throbbings through the lands, and gave them
Such a new pulse of nobler life : and when
Their sumless Venture wreckt, and o'er them roll'd
The wormwood waters of defeat and death,
How in their pleading hands they held the Babe
And Orphan Liberty, and bade her rear it
For love of them, and for its own sweet sake.
And England slinks behind the nations now.
Dim is her Beacon Despots paled to see
Burn on them through the dark, like God's stern eye.
Her battle-armour rusteth in her halls,
And the old mighty arm that struck such blows
For Right and Freedom, hangeth listless now.

A dry-rot eats her life: her God is Mammon!
God Mars no longer leaps into her heart,
As in a chariot driving down to battle.
Her ancient fame and valour have become
A tale that's told us of forgotten times—
Some fabled Kraken slumbering in its sea!
O! for the voice of Milton once again,
To make the lion-eyes lighten, and her heart
As tremblingly alive as is a Star,
Till in her naked strength majestical
She walkt the sun-road of her glorious way.
But England sleeps—the Ruin still rolls on.
Earth crouches 'neath the shuddering wings of Fear.
Silent, and very calm, Freedom lies husht,
And listens like a panting thing pursued,
Hearkening, heart-stifled, for the stealthiest tread
Of One that hunts like Tarquin for Lucrece.
'Tis midnight now, and all the creeping things,
And Birds of Darkness, ply their ghastly work.
Life gropes and stumbles among gaping graves,
And Freedom's worshippers fall headless, while
They bend to give their hearts up at her shrine!
But God's in heaven, and yet the Day shall dawn—
Break from the dark upon her golden wings,
Her quick, ripe splendours rend and burn the gloom,
Her living tides of glory burst, and foam,
And hurry along the darken'd streets of night.
Cloud after cloud shall light a rainbow-roof,

And build a Triumph-Arch for conquering Day
To flash her beauty—trail her grandeurs through,
And take the World in her white arms of light.
And earth shall fling aside her mask of gloom,
And lift her tearful face. O there will be
Blood on it thick as dews! The Children's blood
Splasht in the Mother's face! And there must be
A red sunrise of retribution yet!
A mighty future is about to break
The hush o' the world—the waiting gloom in heaven.
The New Year cometh with a magic key,
To ope some radiant chamber in Time's palace.
Our Martyrs have not sworn such seed in vain!
Beneath old Winter's snows a world of hope
Lies ripening, and shall richly run to flowers,
When Spring comes dancing like a jubilant Psaltress,
And free earth kindles as a countenance
Alive with love, and all the soul alight!
O come, thou Spring of God, and at thy voice
The balmy blood shall beat in bud and leaf!
And come, thou mellow rain, fall on it warm,
And fondle it with kisses, drop rich tears;
And blow, thou sweet Spring-wind, and set it stirring
With secret rapture—budding tenderly,
With all the glory of its folded bloom,
And all its fragrance striving for the light.
God, what a Spring and Harvest yet shall crown
The dark, dern Deluge of Calamity!

Then come, thou grand New Year, in silence come
Across the white snows, and the winter-land.
Come, great Deliverer, call the peoples up,—
Up from the Egypt of their slavery !
Ring out the death-knell of old Tyranny—
'Tis rotten ripe, and the heart of half the world
Doth beat and burst to hurry it into hell.
Stride o'er the Present, grand as some huge wave
Should rush across Panama at a leap,
And make two Seas one perfect world of waters.
So link our great Past to a nobler Future,
And set our new world singing on its way,
With sunshine freighted, like a heart of bliss,
Her Life's rich tide at Glory's high flood-mark.
A little while, and we shall yet return
Each to the Fatherland, like kings to conquest.
Light breaks there ! in the East : it grows, and soon
Shall Freedom's sun roll up the Heaven of Life.
We may not see God's face, yet at our side
He combats for us, with his vizor down.
But no words—like weeds they sap the soul
Of richness that should fill the fruit of deeds.
Henceforth let lips be dumb, as Bravery—
Her parley done—had shut her gates, to ope not
Save for the shouts that chariot Victory forth.
We are all ready ! We have waited long !
God strike the hour, Ho ! let the trumpets ring !"
He ceased. One shout ran thro' the night, and struck

Heaven's boss of stars, and like a ship went down
In the lone sea of silence flowing round.
In touching majesty the Stars lookt down,
As tho' they yearn'd to them with answering pulse,
And with invisible speed the world roll'd on.

---

## SONG.

Like leaves from Autumn's bough, Old Friend,
Our ripest hopes depart ;
And there's little left us now, Old Friend,
To cheer the Patriot's heart.
The Altars where we knelt, Old Friend,
Grow desolate and cold,
And faint is the faith we felt, Old Friend,
I' the valiant days of old.

In bloody shrouds they sleep, Old Friend,
Who could not live as slaves :
And the living only weep, Old Friend,
Above their Martyrs' graves !
Freedom hath many a wound, Old Friend,
And, ring'd by hounds of hell,
She wraps her purple round, Old Friend,
To fall as Cæsar fell.

The men of blood prevail, Old Friend,
And, stricken in the night,
The people's weeping wail, Old Friend,
Goes praying for the light.
And yet their day shall come, Old Friend,
Though we may never hear
The shouts of Harvest-home, Old Friend,
Nor see the golden year.

---

O THE white Snow crowns the Hills, and the arms of Ether fills,
In the glory of its loveliness—a presence as of light,
And it looks up in Heaven's face with all a Virgin's trusting grace:
So the Maiden walkt on Purity's white height.
But the Snow will blush for bliss, at the red Dawn's fervent kiss;
And fall from its high throne, and lose the brightness from its brow;
And be trodden on the highways, and be trampled in the byways:
So the Maiden's life is stain'd and trampled now.

## EIGHTEEN HUNDRED AND FORTY-EIGHT.

PEOPLE of England, rouse ye from your dreaming !
  Sinew your souls for Freedom's glorious leap :
Look to the Future, where our day-spring's gleaming :
  Lo ! a pulse stirs that never more shall sleep
In the world's heart. Men's eyes flash wide with wonder!
  The Robbers tremble in their mightiest tower,
Strange words roll o'er their souls with wheels of thunder,
  The leaves from Royalty's tree fall hour by hour,—
  Earthquakes leap in our Temples, crumbling Throne and Power.

Vampyres have drain'd the human heart's best blood,
  Kings robb'd, and Priests have curst us in God's name:
Out in the midnight of the Past we've stood—
  While fiends of darkness plied their hellish game.
We have been worshipping a gilded crown,
  Which drew heaven's lightning-laughter on our head ;
Chains fell on us as we were bowing down ;
  We deem'd our Gods divine, but lo ! instead—
  They are but painted clay,—with morn the charm has fled !

And this is merry England,—cradling-place
  Of souls self-deified and glory-crown'd !
Where smiles made splendour in the Peasant's face,
  And Justice reign'd—her awful eyes close-bound !
Where Toil with open brow went on light-hearted,
  And twain in love Law never thrust apart ?
How is the glory of our life departed
  From us, who sit and nurse our bleeding smart :
  And slink, afraid to break the laws that break the
        heart !

Husht be the Herald on the walls of fame,
  Trumping this People as their Country's pride ;
Weep rather, with your souls on fire with shame :
  See ye not how the palaced knaves deride
Us flatter'd fools ? how priestcraft, strong and stealthy,
  Stabs at our freedom through its veil of night,
And grinds the poor to flush its coffers wealthy ?
  Hear how the land groans in the grip of Might,
  Then quaff your cup of Wrongs, and laud a Briton's
        "Right."

There's not a spot in all this flowery land,
  Where Tyranny's cursed brand-mark has not been :
O ! were it not for its all-blasting hand,
  Dear Christ, what a sweet heaven this might have been !

Has it not hunted forth our spirits brave,—
   Kill'd the red rose of health which crown'd our daughters,
Wedded our living hopes unto the grave,—
   Filled happy homes with strife, the world with slaughters,
   And turn'd our thoughts to blood—to gall, the heart's sweet waters?

Where is the spirit of our ancient Sires?
   Who, bleeding, wrung their Rights from tyrannies olden.
God-spirits have been here, for Freedom fires
   From out their ashes, to earth's heart enfolden;
The mighty dead lie slumbering around,—
   Whose names thrill thro' us as Gods were in the air:
Life leaps from where their dust makes holy ground;
   Their deeds spring forth in glory,—live all-where,—
   But we are traitors to the trust they bade us bear.

Go forth, when Night is husht, and heaven is clothéd
   With smiling stars that in God's presence roll,
Feel the stirr'd spirit leap to them betrothéd,
   As Angel-wings were fanning in the soul;
Feel the hot tears flood in the eyes upturning,
   The tide of goodness heave its brightest waves,—
Then suddenly crush the grand and God-ward yearning

With the mad thought that ye are bounden slaves !
O! how long will ye make your hearts its living graves !

Immortal Liberty ! we see thee stand
Like Morn just stept from heaven upon a mountain
With beautiful feet, and blessing-laden hand,
And heart that welleth Love's most living fountain !
O! when wilt thou string on the People's lyre
Joy's broken chord ! And on the People's brow
Set Empire's crown ? Light up thy beacon-fire
Within their hearts, with an undying glow ;
Nor give us blood for milk, as men are drunk with now ?

Curst, curst be war, the World's most fatal glory !
Ye wakening nations, burst its guilty thrall !
Time waits with out-stretcht hand to shroud the gory
Grim glaive of strife behind Oblivion's pall.
The Tyrant laughs at swords, the cannon's rattle
Thunders no terror on his murderous soul.
Thought, Mind, must conquer Might, and in this battle
The Warrior's cuirass, or the Sophist's stole,
Shall blunt no lance of light, no onset backward roll.

Old Poets tell us of a golden age,
When earth was guiltless,—Gods the guests of men,
Ere sin had dimm'd the heart's illumined page,—
And Sinai-voices say 'twill come again.

O! happy age! when Love shall rule the heart,
And time to live shall be the poor man's dower,
When Martyrs bleed no more, nor Exiles smart—
Mind is the only diadem of power—
People, it ripens now! awake! and strike the hour.

Hearts, high and mighty, gather in our cause.
Bless, bless, O God, and crown their earnest labour,
Who dauntless fight to win us equal laws,
With mental armour, and with spirit-sabre!
Bless, bless, O God! the proud intelligence,
That like a sun dawns on the People's forehead,—
Humanity springs from them like incense,
The Future burst upon them, boundless—starried,—
They weep repentant tears, that they so long have tarried.

---

## THE PATRIOT.

Ay, Tyrants, build your Babels! forge your fetters! link your chains!
As brims your guilt-cup fuller, ours of grief ebbs to the drains:

Still, as on Christ's brow, crowns of thorn for Freedom's
Martyrs twine ;
Still batten on live hearts, and madden, o'er the hot blood-
wine.
Murder men sleeping, or awake,—torture them dumb
with pain,
And tear, with hands all bloody red, Mind's jewels from
the brain!
Your feet are on us, Tyrants—strike ! and hush Earth's
wail of sorrow :
Your sword of power, so red to-day, shall kiss the dust
to-morrow.
O ! but 'twill be a merry day, the world shall set apart,
When Strife's last brand is broken in the last crown'd
Tyrant's heart!
And it shall come,—despite of Rifle, Rope, and Rack,
and Scaffold,
Once more we ilft the earnest brow, and battle on un-
baffled.

Our hopes ran mountains high, we sang at heart, wept
tears of gladness,
When France, the bravely beautiful, dasht down her scep-
tred madness ;
And Hungary her one-hearted race of mighty heroes
hurl'd
In the death-grip of the nations, as a bulwark for the
world.

O Hungary! gallant Hungary! grand and glorious thou
wert,
The World's soul feeling, like a river, gushing from God's
heart:
And Rome,—who, while her Heroes bled, felt her old
breast heave higher,
How her eyes redden'd with the flash of all their Roman
fire!
Mothers of children, who shall live the Gods of future
story!
Your blood shall blossom from the dust, and crown the
world with glory.
Ye'll tread them down yet! curse and crown, Czar,
Kaiser, King and slave,
And Freedom shall be sovran in the courts of fool and
knave

Wail for the hopes that have gone down! the young life
vainly spilt!
Th' Eternal Murder still sits crown'd, and throned in
damning guilt.
Still in God's golden sun the Tyrants' bloody banners
burn,
And Priests,—Hell's midnight Thugs!—to their soul-
strangling work return!

See how the oppressors of the poor with serpents hunt our
blood ;
Hear, from the dark, the groan and curse go maddening
up to God.
They kill and trample us poor worms, till earth is dead
men's dust ;
Death's red tooth daily drains our hearts, but end, ay,
end it must.
The herald of our coming Christ leaps in the womb of
Time ;
The poor's grand army treads the Age's march with step
sublime.
Ours is the mighty future! and what marvel, brother men,
If the devoured of ages should turn devourers then ?

O! brothers of the bounding heart, I look thro' tears and
smile,
Our land is rife with sounds of fetters snapping 'neath the
file ;
I lay my hand on England's heart, and in each life-throb
mark,
The pealing thought of freedom ring its Tocsin in the
dark.
I see the Toiler hath become a glorious Christ-like preacher,
And, as he wins a crust, stands proudly forth, the great
world-teacher ;

He still toils on, but, Tyrants, 'tis a mighty thing when slaves,
Who delve their lives into their work, know that they delve your graves.
Anarchs! your doom comes swiftly! brave and eagle spirits climb,
To ring Oppression's death-knell from the old watch-towers of time;
A spirit of Cromwellian might is stirring at this hour,
And thought is burning in men's eyes with more than speechful power.

Old England, cease the mummer's part! wake, Starveling, Serf, and Slave!
Rouse in the majesty of wrong, great kindred of the brave!
Speak, and the world shall answer, with her voices myriad fold,
And men, like Gods, shall grapple with the giant-wrongs of old.
Now, Mothers of the people, give your babes heroic milk;
Sires, soul your sons to daring deeds, no more soft words of silk;
Great spirits of the mighty dead take shape, and walk our mind,
Their glory smites our upward look, we seem no longer blind;

They tell us how they broke their bonds, and whisper, "So may ye,"
One sharp, stern struggle, and the slaves of centuries are free!
The people's heart, with pulse like cannon, panteth for the fray,
And, brothers, gallant brothers, we'll be with you in that day.

---

## A LOVER'S FANCY.

Sweet Heaven! I do love a maiden,
Radiant, rare, and beauty-laden:
When she's near me, heaven is round me,
Her dear presence doth so bound me!
I could wring my heart of gladness,
Might it free her lot of sadness!
Give the world, and all that's in it,
Just to press her hand a minute!
Yet she weeteth not I love her;
  Never dare I tell the sweet
Tale, but to the stars above her,
  And the flowers that kiss her feet.

O! to live and linger near her,
And in tearful moments cheer her!

I could be a Bird to lighten
Her dear heart,—her sweet eyes brighten:
Or in fragrance, like a blossom,
Give my life up on her bosom!
For my love's withouten measure,
All its pangs are sweetest pleasure;
Yet she weeteth not I love her;
  Never dare I tell the sweet
Tale, but to the stars above her,
  And the flowers that kiss her feet.

---

## SONG.

All glorious as a Rainbow's birth,
  She came in Spring-tide's golden hours;
When Heaven went hand-in-hand with Earth,
  And May was crown'd with buds and flowers!
The mounting devil at my heart
  Clomb faintlier as my life did win
The charméd heaven, she wrought apart,
  To wake its slumbering Angel in!
With radiant mien she trode serene,
  And past me smiling by!
O! who that lookt could chance but love?
  Not I, sweet soul, not I.

Her budding breasts, like fragrant fruit,
  Peer'd out, a-yearning to be prest:
Her voice shook all my heart's red root!
  Yet might not break a babe's soft rest!
Her being mingled into mine,
  As breath of flowers doth mix and melt,
And on her lips the honey-wine
  Was royal-rich as spikenard spilt;
With love a-gush, like water-brooks,
  Her heart smiled in her eye;
O! who that lookt could chance but love?
  Not I, sweet soul, not I.

The dewy eyelids of the Dawn
  Ne'er oped such heaven as hers can show:
O Love! such eyes have surely shone
  As jewels in some starry brow!
Her brow flasht glory like a shrine,
  Or lily-bell with sunburst bright;
Where came and went love-thoughts divine,
  As low winds walk the leaves in light:
She wore her beauty with the grace
  Of Summer's star-clad sky;
O! who that lookt could chance but love?
  Not I, sweet soul, not I.

## IT WILL END IN THE RIGHT.

NEVER despair ! O, my Brother in sorrow !
I know that our mourning is ended not. Yet,
Shall the vanquisht to-day be the victors to-morrow,
Our Star shall shine on when the Tyrant's sun's set.
Hold on! tho' they spurn thee, for whom thou art living
A life only cheer'd by the lamp of its love :
Hold on ! Freedom's hope to the bounden ones giving :
Green spots in the waste wait the worn spirit-dove ;
Hold on,—still hold on,—in the world's despite,
Nurse the faith in thy heart, keep the lamp of God bright,
And, my life for thine ! it shall end in the Right.

What, tho' the Martyrs and Prophets have perisht ?
The Angel of Life rolls the stone from their graves :
Immortal's the love, and the freedom they cherisht,
Their Faith's Triumph-cry stirs the spirits of slaves !
They are gone,—but a Glory is left in our life,
Like the day-god's last kiss on the darkness of Even—
Gone down on the desolate seas of their strife,
To climb as star-beacons up Liberty's heaven.
Hold on,—still hold on,—in the world's despite,
Nurse the faith in thy heart, keep the lamp of God bright,
And, my life for thine ! it shall end in the Right.

Think of the Wrongs that have ground us for ages,
  Think of the Wrongs we have still to endure!
Think of our blood red on History's pages;
  Then work, that our reck'ning be speedy and sure.
Slaves, cry unto God! but be our God reveal'd
  In our lives, in our works, in our warfare for man;
And bearing—or borne upon—Victory's shield,
  Let us fight battle-harness'd, and fall in the van.
Hold on,—still hold on,—in the world's despite,
Nurse the faith in thy heart, keep the lamp of God bright,
And, my life for thine! it shall end in the Right.

---

## GOD'S WORLD IS WORTHY BETTER MEN.

Behold! an idle tale they tell,
  And who shall blame their telling it?
The rogues have got their cant to sell,
  The world pays well for selling it!
They say the world's a desert drear,—
  Still plagued with Egypt's blindness!
That we were sent to suffer here,—
  What! by a God of kindness?
That since the world has gone astray,
  It must be so for ever,

And we should stand still, and obey
Its Desolators. Never!
We'll labour for the better time,
With all our might of Press and Pen;
Believe me, 'tis a truth sublime,
God's world is worthy better men.

With Paradise the world began,
A world of love and gladness:
Its beauty may be marr'd by man
With all his crime and madness,
Yet 'tis a brave world still. Love brings
A sunshine for the dreary;
With all our strife, sweet Rest hath wings
To fold o'er hearts a-weary.
The Sun in glory, like a God,
To-day climbs up heaven's bosom,
The flowers upon the jewell'd sod
In sweet love-lessons blossom,
As radiant of immortal youth
And beauty, as in Eden; then
Believe me, 'tis a noble truth,
God's world is worthy better men.

O! they are bold, knaves over-bold,
Who say we are doom'd to anguish:
That men in God's own image soul'd,
Like hell-bound slaves, must languish.

Probe Nature's heart to its red core,
  There's more of good than evil ;
And man, down-trampled man, is more
  Of Angel than of Devil.
Prepare to die ? *Prepare to live !*
  We know not what is living :
And let us for the world's good give,
  As God is ever giving.
Give Action, Thought, Love, Wealth, and Time,
  To win the primal age again ;
Believe me, 'tis a truth sublime,
  God's world is worthy better men.

---

## OLD ENGLAND.

THERE she sits in her Island-home,
    Peerless among her Peers !
And Humanity oft to her arms doth come,
    To ease its poor heart of tears.
Old England still throbs with the muffled fire
    Of a Past she can never forget :
And again shall she banner the world up higher ;
    For there's life in the Old Land yet.

They would mock at her now, who of old lookt forth
In their fear, as they heard her afar ;
But loud will your wail be, O Kings of the Earth!
When the Old Land goes down to the war.
The Avalanche trembles half-launcht, and half-riven,
Her voice will in motion set :
O ring out the tidings, ye Winds of heaven !
There's life in the Old Land yet.

The old nursing Mother's not hoary yet,
There is sap in her Saxon tree ;—
Lo ! she lifteth a bosom of glory yet,
Thro' her mists to the Sun and the Sea.
Fair as the Queen of Love, fresh from the foam,
Or a Star in a dark cloud set;
Ye may blazon her shame,—ye may leap at her name,—
But there' life in the Old Land yet.

Let the storm burst, it will find the Old Land
Ready-ripe for a rough, red fray !
She will fight as she fought when she took her stand,
For the Right in the olden day.
Ay, rouse the old royal soul, Europe's best hope
Is her sword-edge by Victory set !
She shall dash Freedom's foes adown Death's bloody slope ;
For there's life in the Old Land yet.

## A POOR MAN'S WIFE.

HER dainty hand nestled in mine, rich and white,
  And timid as trembling dove :
And it twinkled about me, a jewel of light,
  As she garnisht our feast of love ;
'T was the queenliest hand in all lady-land,
  And she was a poor Man's wife !
O ! but little ye'd think how that wee, white hand
  Could dare in the battle of Life.

Her heart it was lowly as maiden's might be,
  But hath climb'd to heroic height,
And burn'd like a shield in defence of me,
  On the sorest field of fight !
And startling as fire, it hath often flasht up
  In her eyes, the good heart and rare !
As she drank down her half of our bitterest cup,
  And taught me how to bear.

Her sweet eyes that seem'd, with their smile sublime,
  Made to look me and light me to heaven,
They have triumph'd thro' bitter tears many a time,
  Since their love to my life was given :

And the maiden-meek voice of the womanly Wife
  Still bringeth the heavens nigher ;
For it rings like the voice of God over my life,
  Aye bidding me climb up higher.

I hardly dared think it was human, when
  I first lookt in her yearning face ;
For it shone as the heavens had open'd then,
  And clad it with glory and grace !
But dearer its light of healing grew
  In our dark and desolate day,
As the Rainbow, when heav'n hath no break of blue,
  Smileth the storm away.

O! her shape was the lithest Loveliness,—
  Just an armful of heav'n to unfold !
But the form that bends flower-like in love's caress,
  With the Victor's strength is soul'd !
In her worshipful presence transfigur'd I stand,
  And the poor Man's English home
She lights with the Beauty of Greece the grand,
  And the glory of regallest Rome.

## LINES INSCRIBED TO THE REV. F. D. MAURICE.

God bless you, Brave One, in our dearth,
  Your life shall leave a trailing glory;
And round the poor Man's homely hearth
  We proudly tell your suffering's story.

All Saviour-souls have sacrificed,
  With nought but noble faith for guerdon;
And ere the world hath crown'd the Christ,
  The man to death hath borne the burden!

The Savage broke the glass that brought
  The heavens nearer, saith the legend!
Even so the Bigots welcome aught
  That makes our vision starrier region'd!

They lay their Corner-stones in dark
  Deep waters, who up-build in beauty,
On Earth's old heart, their Triumph-Arc
That crowns with glory lives of duty.

And meekly still the Martyrs go
  To keep with Pain their solemn bridal!
And still they walk the fire who bow
  Not down to worship Custom's Idol.

In fieriest forge of martyrdom,
  Their swords of soul must weld and brighten:
Tear-bathed, from fiercest furnace, come
  Their lives, heroic-tempered—Titan!

And heart-strings sweetest music make
  When swept by Suffering's fiery fingers!
And thro' soul-shadows starriest break
  The glories on God's brave light-bringers.

Take heart! tho' sown in tears and blood,
  No seed that's quick with love, hath perisht,
Tho' dropt in barren byeways—God
  Some glorious flower of life hath cherisht.

Take heart; the rude dust dark To-day,
  Soars a new-lighted sphere To-morrow!
And wings of splendour burst the clay
  That clasps us in Death's fruitful furrow.

## LOVE.

O Love ! Love ! Love !
Its glory smites our gloom,
And flower-like flusht with life, the heart
Doth burgeon into bloom !
Sweet as the sunshine's golden-kiss,
That crowns the world anew :
Sweet as in Roses' hearts of bliss,
Soft, summer-dark, drops dew.

O Love ! Love ! Love !
May make the brave heart ache ;
Pulse out its lavish life, and leave
It, mournfully to break !
But O how exquisite it starts
The thoughts that bee-like cling,
To drain the honey from young hearts,
And brave a bleeding sting !

O Love ! Love ! Love !
Its very pain endears !
And every wail and weeping brings
Some blessing on our tears !

Love makes our darkest days, sweet dove!
  In golden Suns go down,
And still we'll clothe our hearts with love,
  And crown us with Love's crown.

---

## A SONG IN THE CITY.

Coining the heart, brain, and sinew, to gold,
  Till we sink in the dark, on the pauper's dole,
Feeling for ever the flowerless mould,
  Growing about the uncrowned soul!
O, God! O, God! must this evermore be
The lot of the Children of Poverty?
  The spring is calling from brae and bower,
  In the twinkling sheen of the sunny hour,
    Earth smiles in her golden green;
Glad as the bird in tree-top chanting
    Its anthem of Liberty!
With its heart in its musical gratitude panting,
    And O, 'tis a bliss to be!
Once more to drink in the life-breathing air,
  Lapt in luxurious flowers—
To recall again the pleasures that were
  In Infancy's innocent hours—

To wash the earth-stains and the dust from my soul,
  In nature's reviving tears, once more ;
To feast at her banquet, and drink from her bowl
  Rich dew, for the heart's hot core.
Ah me ! ah me ! it is heavenly then,
  And hints of the spirit-world, near alway,
Are stirring, and stirred, at my heart again,
  Like leaves to the kiss of May :
It is but a dream, yet' tis passing sweet,
  And when from its spells my spirit is waking,
Dark as my heart, and the wild tears start ;
  FOR I WAS NOT MADE MERELY FOR MONEY-MAKING.

  My soul leaneth out, to the whisperings
  Of the mighty, the marvellous spirits of old ;
And heaven-ward soareth to strengthen her wings,
  When Labour relapseth its earthly hold ;
And breathless with awfullest beauty—it listens,
  To catch the Night's deep, starry mystery;
Or in mine eyes, dissolved, glistens,
  Big, for the moan of Humanity.
Much that is written within its chamber,
Much that is shrined in the mind's living amber,
    Much of this thought of mine,
  There's music below, in the glistering leaves,
  There's music above, and heaven's blue bosom heaves
    The silvery clouds between ;

The boughs of the woodland are nodding in play,
And wooingly beckon my spirit away—
I hear the dreamy hum
Of bees in the lime-tree, and birds on the spray;
And they, too, are calling my thinking away ;
But I cannot—cannot come.
Vision of verdant and heart-cooling places
Will steal on my soul like a golden spring-rain.
Bringing the lost light of brave, vanisht faces ;
Till all my life blossoms with beauty again.
But O, for a glimpse of the flower-laden Morning,
That makes the heart leap up, and knock at heaven's door !
O for the green lane, the green field, the green wood,
To take in, by heartfuls, their greenness once more !
How I yearn to lie down in the lush-flower'd meadows,
And nestle in leaves, and the sleep of the shadows,
Where violets in the cool gloom are awaking,
There, let my soul burst from its cavern of clay,
To float down the warm spring, away and away!
For I was not made merely for money-making.

At my wearisome task I oftentimes turn
From my bride, and my monitress, Duty,
Forgetting the strife, and the wrestle of life,
To talk with the spirit of beauty,
The multitude's hum, and the chinking of gold,
Grow hush as the dying of day,

For on wings, pulsing music, with joy untold,
  My heart is up, and away!
I fain would struggle and give to birth ;
For I would not pass away from earth,
      And make no sign !
I yearn to utter, what might live on,
In the world's heart, when I am gone.
I would not plod on, like these slaves of gold,
  Who shut up their souls, in a dusky cave :
I would see the world better, and nobler-soul'd,
  Ere I dream of heaven in my green turf-grave.
I may toil till my life is filled with dreariness,
Toil till my heart is a wreck in its weariness,
Toil for ever, for tear-steept bread,
Till I go down to the silent dead.
But, by this yearning, this hoping, this aching,
I WAS NOT MADE MERELY FOR MONEY-MAKING.

---

## A WELCOME TO LOUIS KOSSUTH.

Ho ! Patriots of old England, wake !
  And join ye heart and hand,
To welcome him for Freedom's sake
  Within our fatherland !

He needs no proud triumphal arch,
  Nor banners on the wind :
In hearts that beat his triumph-march,
  Our Kossuth's fitly shrined !
We meet him here, we greet him here—
  With Love's wide arms caress him !
And Kings have no such welcome dear,
  As Kossuth hath : *God bless him.*

He rose like Freedom's morning star,
  Where all was darkling, dim—
We saw his glory from afar,
  And fought in soul for him !
Brave Victor ! how his radiant brow
  King'd Freedom's host like Saul !
And in his crown of sorrow now
  He's royallest heart of all.
We meet him here, we greet him here—
  With Love's wide arms caress him !
And Kings have no such welcome dear,
  As Kossuth hath : *God bless him.*

Ay, English hearts thro' proud tears gush
  With glory at his name—
Whose brave deeds made the roused blood rush
  Along our veins like flame :

We cheer'd him thro' his hero-strife—
  And, in his presence met,
We'll show the world that noble life
  Lives in Old England yet!
We meet him here, we greet him here—
  With Love's wide arms caress him!
And King's have no such welcome dear,
  As Kossuth hath: *God bless him.*

He cometh dim with glorious dust,
  From out his wrestling ring:
But, blessings—praises—deathless trust—
  Like armies round him cling!
And Freedom runs her radiant round,
  Tho' clouds shut out the sky;
And soon the World's great heart shall bound
  To Kossuth's conquering cry.
We meet him here, we greet him here—
  With Love's wide arms caress him!
And Kings have no such welcome dear,
  As Kossuth hath: *God bless him.*

His Hungary billows o'er with graves
  Of Martyrs not in vain:
See what a ripening harvest waves
  Its fruit of that red rain!

Again his flaming sword shall glare.
  The Despots' splendour dim :
And palsy strike the arm that dare
  Not strike a blow for him !
We meet him here, we greet him here—
  With Love's wide arms caress him !
And Kings have no such welcome dear,
  As Kossuth hath : *God bless him.*

Ring out, exult, and clap your hands,
  Free Men and Women brave—
Shout, Britain ! shake the startled lands,
  And free the bounden Slave !
Come forth, make merry in the sun,
  And give him welcome due ;
Heroic hearts have crown'd him one
  Of Earth's Immortal few !
We meet him here, we greet him here—
  With Love's wide arms caress him !
And Kings have no such welcome dear,
  As Kossuth hath : *God bless him.*

## ONWARD AND SUNWARD.

TELL me the song of the beautiful Stars,
As grandly they glide on their blue way above us,
Looking, despite of our spirit's sin-scars,
Down on us tenderly, yearning to love us!
This is the song in their work-worship sung,
Down thro' the world-jewelled universe rung:
"Onward for ever, for evermore onward,"
And ever they open their loving eyes Sunward.

"Onward," shouts Earth, with her myriad voices
Of music, aye answering the song of the Seven,
As like a wing'd child of God's love she rejoices,
Swinging her censer of glory in heaven.
And lo, it is writ by the finger of God,
In sunbeams and flowers on the live-green sod:
Onward for ever, for evermore onward,
And ever she turneth all trustfully Sunward.

The mightiest souls of all time hover o'er us,
Who labour'd like gods among men, and have gone
Like great bursts of sun on the dark way before us:
They're with us, still with us, our battle fight on,

Looking down victor-brow'd, from the glory-crown'd hill
They beckon, and beacon us, on, onward still :
And the true heart's aspirings are onward, still onward ;
It turns to the Future, as earth turneth Sunward.

---

## A MAIDEN'S SONG.

I LOVE ! and Love hath given me
    Sweet thoughts to God akin
And oped a living Paradise
    My heart of hearts within :
O from this Eden of my life
    God keep the Serpent Sin !

I love ! and into angel-land
    With starry glimpses peer !
I drink in beauty like heaven-wine,
    When One is smiling near !
And there's a Rainbow round my soul
    For every falling tear.

Dear God in heaven ! keep without stain
    My bosom's brooding Dove :
O clothe it meet for angel-arms,

And give it place above !
For there is nothing from the world
I yearn to take, but Love.

---

## THERE'S NO DEARTH OF KINDNESS.

THERE'S no dearth of kindness
  In this world of ours ;
Only in our blindness
  We gather thorns for flowers !
Outward, we are spurning—
  Trampling one another ?
While we are inly yearning
  At the name of "Brother !"

There's no dearth of kindness
  Or love among mankind,
But in darkling loneness
  Hooded hearts grow blind !
Full of kindness tingling,
  Soul is shut from soul,
When they might be mingling
  In one kindred whole !

There's no dearth of kindness,
  Tho' it be unspoken,
From the heart it buildeth
  Rainbow-smiles in token—
That there be none so lowly,
  But have some angel-touch :
Yet, nursing loves unholy,
  We live for self too much !

As the Wild-rose bloweth,
  As runs the happy river,
Kindness freely floweth
  In the heart for ever.
But if men will hanker
  Ever for golden dust,
Kingliest hearts will canker,
  Brightest spirits rust.

There's no dearth of kindness
  In this world of ours ;
Only in our blindness
  We gather thorns for flowers !
O cherish God's best giving,
  Falling from above !
Life were not worth living,
  Were it not for Love.

## A LYRIC OF LOVE.

The Lark that nestles nearest earth,
To Heaven's gate nighest sings;
And loving thee, my lowly life
Doth mount on Lark-like wings!
Thine eyes are starry promises:
And affluent above
All measure in its blessing, is
The largess of thy love.

Merry as laughter 'mong the hills,
Spring dances at my heart!
And at my wooing Nature's soul,
Into her face will start!
The Queen-moon, in her starry bower
Looks happier for our love;
A dewier splendour fills the flower,
And mellower coos the Dove.

My heart may sometimes blind mine eyes
With utterance of tears,
But feels no pang for thee, Belov'd!
But all the more endears:

And if life comes with cross and care
  Unknown in years of yore,
I know thou 'lt half the burden bear,
  And I am strong once more.

Ah ! now I see my life was shorn,
  That, like the forest-brook
When leaves are shed, my darkling soul
  Up in heaven's face might look !
And blessings on the storm that gave
  Me haven on thy breast,
Where life hath climaxt like a wave
  That breaks in perfect rest.

---

## THE FAMINE-SMITTEN.

In the tears of the Morning—
    The smiles of the sun,
The green Earth's adorning
    Told spring had begun !
Warm woods donn'd their beauty, wrought
    Through long still nights,
And musical breezes brought
    Flowery delights :

The humming leaves flasht
    Rich in light, with sweet sound,
And the glad waters dasht
    Their starry spray round!
The wood-bines up-climbing,
    Laught out, pink-and-golden,
And bees made sweet chiming
    In roses half-folden,
But where was that infant-band,
    Wont in spring weather
To wander forth, hand-in-hand,
    Violets to gather?
Ah misery! they slept,
    The dear blossoms of lòve!
Where the green branches wept,
    And the grass crept above;
Melodious gladness
    Throbb'd thro' the rich air,
But the anguish of madness
    Rent Poverty's lair;
For Famine had smitten
    Its pride of life low,
And agony written
    On heart and on brow.
Sweet from the boughs the birds
    Sang in their mirth,
The lark messaged heaven-wards
    Blessings from earth—

But I turn'd where our gentle Lord's
Loves lay in dearth.
They heard not, nor heeded,
The sounds of life o'er them !
They felt not, nor needed,
The hot tears wept for them !
But earth-flowers were springing
O'er human flowers' grave,
And, O God ! what heart-wringing
Their tender looks gave !
They died ! died of hunger—
By bitter want blasted !
While wealth for the Wronger
Ran over untasted—
While Pomp, in joy's rosy bow'rs,
Wasted life's measure,
Chiding the lagging hours,
Wearied of pleasure !
They died ! while men hoarded
The free gifts of God :
They died ! 'tis recorded
In letters of blood.
Yet the corn on the hills
Waves its showery-gold crown ;
Still Nature's lap fills
With the good heaven drops down.
O ! this world might be lighted
With Eden's first smile—

Angel-haunted—unblighted,
With freedom for Toil :
But they wring out our blood
For their banquet of gold !
They annul laws of God,
Soul and body are sold !
Hark now ! hall and palace,
Ring out, dome and rafter !
Ay, laugh on, ye callous !
In Hell there'll be laughter :
But tremble, hell-makers ;
The shorn among men—
The world's image-breakers
Grow mighty again ;
There be stern times a-coming,
The dark days of reck'ning,
The storms are up-looming—
The Nemesis wak'ning !
On heaven, blood shall call,
Earth quake with pent thunder,
And shackle and thrall
Shall be riven asunder.
It will come, it shall come,
Impede it what may :
Up, People ! and welcome
Your glorious day !

## OUR FATHERS ARE PRAYING FOR PAUPER PAY.

SMITTEN stones will talk with fiery tongues,
  And the worm, when trodden, will turn;
But, Cowards, ye cringe to the cruellest wrongs,
  And answer with never a spurn.
Then torture, O Tyrants, the spiritless drove,
  Old England's Helots will bear:
There's no hell in their hatred, no God in their love,
  Nor shame in their dearth's despair.
For our Fathers are praying for Pauper-pay,
  Our Mother's with Death's kiss are white;
Our Sons are the rich man's Serfs by day,
  And our Daughters his Slaves by night.

The Tearless are drunk with our tears: have they driven
  The God of the poor man mad?
For we weary of waiting the help of Heaven,
  And the battle goes still with the bad.
O but death for death, and life for life,
  It were better to take and give,
With hand to throat, and knife to knife,
  Than die out as thousands live!

For our Fathers are praying for Pauper-pay,
Our Mothers with Death's kiss are white;
Our Sons are the rich man's Serfs by day,
And our Daughters his Slaves by night.

Fearless and few were the Heroes of old,
Who play'd the peerless part:
We are fifty-fold, but the gangrene Gold
Hath eaten out Hampden's heart.
With their faces to danger, like free-men they fought,
With their daring, all heart and hand:
And the thunder-deed follow'd the lightning-thought,
When they stood for their own good land.
Our Fathers are praying for Pauper-pay,
Our Mothers with Death's kiss are white;
Our Sons are the rich man's Serfs by day,
And our Daughters his Slaves by night.

When the heart of one half the world doth beat
Akin to the brave and the true,
And the tramp of Democracy's earthquake feet
Goes thrilling the wide world through,—
We should not be living in darkness and dust,
And dying like slaves in the night;
But, big with the might of the inward "*must,*"
We should battle for Freedom and Right!

For our Fathers are praying for Pauper-pay,
Our Mothers with Death's kiss are white ;
Our Sons are the rich man's Serfs by day,
And our Daughters his Slaves by night.

---

## A CRY OF THE PEOPLES.

Like a strong man in torture, the weary world turneth,
To clutch Freedom's robe round her slavery's starkness ;
With shame and with shudder, poor mother ; she yearneth
O'er wrongs that are done in her dearth and her darkness.
O gather thy strength up, and crush the Abhorréd,
Who murder thy poor heart, and drain thy life-springs,
And are crownéd to hide the Cain-brand on their forehead :
O let them be last of the Queens and the Kings !

By the lovers and friends we have tenderly cherisht,
Who made the Cause soar up like flame at their breath,
Who struggled like Gods met in fight, and have perisht
In poverty's battle with grim daily death :

O, by all dear ones that bitterly plead for us—
  Life-flowers tied up in the heart's breaking strings—
Sisters that weep for us—mothers that bleed for us—
  Let these be last of the Queens and the Kings !

Sun and Rain kindle greenly the graves of our Martyrs,
  Ye might not tell where the brave blood ran like rain !
But there it burns ever ! and heaven's weeping waters
  And branding suns never shall whiten the stain !
Remember the hurtling the Tyrants have wrought us,
  And smite till each helm bravely flashes and rings !
Life for life, blood for blood, is the lesson they've taught us,
  And be these the last of the Queens and the Kings !

Ho ! weary Nightwatch, is there light on the summit ?
  Yearner up through the Night, say, is there hope ?
For deeper in darkness than fathom of plummet,
  Our Bark thro' the tempest doth stagger and grope !
"To God's unforgiven, to caitiff and craven—
  To Crown and to Sceptre, a cleaving curse clings :
Ye must fling them from deck, would ye steer into heaven,
  For Death tracks the last of the Queens and the Kings !"

## HOPE ON, HOPE EVER.

Hope on, hope ever! though to-day be dark,
  The sweet sunburst may smile on thee to-morrow:
Tho' thou art lonely, there's an eye will mark
  Thy loneliness, and guerdon all thy sorrow!
Tho' thou must toil 'mong cold and sordid men,
  With none to echo back thy thought, or love thee,
Cheer up, poor heart! thou dost not beat in vain,
  For God is over all, and heaven above thee—
          Hope on, hope ever.

The iron may enter in and pierce thy soul,
  But cannot kill the love within thee burning:
The tears of misery, thy bitter dole,
  Can never quench thy true heart's seraph yearning
For better things: nor crush thy ardour's trust,
  That Error from the mind shall be uprooted,
That Truths shall dawn as flowers spring from the dust,
  And Love be cherisht where Hate was embruted!
          Hope on, hope ever.

I know 'tis hard to bear the sneer and taunt,
  With the heart's honest pride at midnight wrestle,
To feel the killing canker-worm of Want,
  While rich rogues in their stolen luxury nestle;

For I have felt it. Yet from Earth's cold Real
  My soul looks out on coming things, and cheerful
The warm Sunrise floods all the land Ideal,
  And still it whispers to the worn and tearful,
      Hope on, hope ever.

Hope on, hope ever! after darkest night,
  Comes, full of loving life, the laughing Morning;
Hope on, hope ever! Spring-tide, flusht with light,
  Aye crowns old Winter with her rich adorning.
Hope on, hope ever! yet the time shall come,
  When man to man shall be a friend and brother;
And this old world shall be a happy home,
  And all Earth's family love one another!
      Hope on, hope ever.

---

## THE PEOPLE'S ADVENT.

'Tis coming up the steep of Time,
  And this old world is growing brighter!
We may not see its dawn sublime,
  Yet high hopes make the heart throb lighter.

We may be sleeping in the ground,
  When it awakes the world in wonder ;
But we have felt it gathering round,
  And heard its voice of living thunder.
      'Tis coming ! yes, 'tis coming !

'Tis coming now, the glorious time,
  Foretold by Seers, and sung in story ;
For which, when thinking was a crime,
  Souls leapt to heaven from scaffolds gory !
They pass'd, nor see the work they wrought,
  Now the crown'd hopes of centuries blossom !
But the live lightning of their thought
  And daring deeds, doth pulse Earth's bosom.
      'Tis coming ! yes, 'tis coming !

Creeds, Empires, Systems, rot with age,
  But the great People's ever youthful !
And it shall write the Future's page,
  To our humanity more truthful !
The gnarliest heart hath tender chords,
  To waken at the name of "Brother ;"
And time comes when brain-scorpion words
  We shall not speak to sting each other.
      'Tis coming ! yes, 'tis coming !

Out of the light, ye Priests, nor fling
  Your dark, cold shadows on us longer !
Aside ! thou world-wide curse, call'd King !
  The People's step is quicker, stronger.
There's a Divinity within
  That makes men great, whene'er they will it.
God works with all who dare to win,
  And the time cometh to reveal it.
        'Tis coming ! yes, 'tis coming !

Freedom ! the tyrants kill thy braves ;
  Yet in our memories live the sleepers,
Tho' murder'd millions feed the graves,
  Dug by Death's fierce, red-handed reapers ;
The world shall not for ever bow
  To things which mock God's own endeavour ;
'Tis nearer than they wot of now,
  When flowers shall wreathe the sword for ever.
        'Tis coming ! yes, 'tis coming !

Fraternity ! Love's other name !
  Dear, heaven-connecting link of Being !
Then shall we grasp thy golden dream,
  As souls, full-statured, grow far-seeing.
Thou shalt unfold our better part,
  And in our Life-cup yield more honey :

Light up with joy the poor man's heart,
  And Love's own world, with smiles more sunny:
          T'is coming ! yes, 'tis coming !

Ay, it must come ! The Tyrant's throne
  Is crumbling with our hot tears rusted ;
The Sword earth's mighty have leant on
  Is canker'd, with our heart's blood crusted.
Room ! for the men of Mind make way!
  Ye robber Rulers, pause no longer ;
Ye cannot stay the opening day :
  The world rolls on, the light grows stronger,—
          The People's Advent 's coming !

---

## KISSES.

One kiss more, Sweet !
Soft as voluptuous wind of the west,
Or silkenest surge of thy purple-vein'd breast,
Ripe lips all ruddily melting apart,
Drink up the honey and wine of my heart !

One kiss more, Sweet !
Warm as a morning sunbeam's dewy gold
Slips in a red Rose's fragrantest fold,

Sets its green blood all a-blush, burning up
At the fresh feel of life, in its crimson cup !

One kiss more, Sweet !
Full as the flush of the sea-waves grand,
Flooding the sheeny fire out of the sand ;
On all the shores of my being let Bliss
Break with its neap-tide sea in a kiss !

---

## PEACE.

Yes, Peace is beautiful ; and I do yearn
For her to clasp the World's poor tortured heart,
As sweet spring warmth doth brood o'er coming flowers.
But peace with these Leviathans of blood—
Who pirate crimson seas, devouring men ?
Give them the hand of brotherhood—whose fangs
Are in our hearts with the grim blood-hound's grip ?
Would'st see Peace, idiot-like, with smirk and smile,
A-planting flowers to coronal Truth's grave ?
Peace, merry-making round the funeral pyre,
Where Freedom, fiery-curtained, weds with death ?
Peace, mirroring her form by pools of blood,—
Crowning the Croat in Vienna's fosse,
With all sweet influences of thankful eyes,

For murder of the glorious Burschenschaft!
Peace with Oppression, which doth tear dear friends
And brothers from our side to-day, and comes
To eat OUR hearts and drink OUR blood to-morrow?
Out on't! it is the Tyrant's cunning cant,
The robe of sheen flung o'er its deadly daggers,
Which start to life, whene'er it hugs to death,
I answer, War!—war with the cause of war,—
War with our misery, want, and wretchedness,—
War with curst Gold, which is an endless war
On Love, and God, and our Humanity!
Brothers, I bid ye forth to glorious war!
Patch fig-leaves o'er the naked truth no more.
The stream of Time runs red with our best blood!
Time's seed-field we have sown with fratricide,
And dragon's teeth have sprung, ay, in our hearts.
O! we have fought and bled on land and sea,
Heapt glory's car with myriads of the brave,
Spilt blood by oceans—treasures by the million,
At every Tyrant's beck. Had we but shed
Such warm and eloquent blood for Freedom's faith,
War's star in heaven had lost its name ere now.
"Brothers!" I cried,—well, Brothers, brother slaves!
O! but to give ye slaves THEIR valiant heart,
Whose dumb, dead dust is worth your living souls—
Dear God! 'twere sweet to kiss the scaffold-block!
I'd proudly leap death's darkness, to let shine
The Future's promise thro' your sorrow's tears!

Sorrow? ah, no! ye feel not sense so holy:
The worm of misery riots in your hearts—
Ye hear your younglings in the drear midnight
Make moan for bread, when ye have none to give!—
Ye drain your life, warm, for the vulture's drink!
The groaning land is choked with living death.
O! ye are mated to the things of scorn,
And I have heard your miserable madness,
Belcht forth in drunken pæans to your tyrants,
Pledging your murderers to the hell they've made!
Ah, Christ! was it for this, thou sudden sun,
Did'st light these centuries with thy dying smile?—
Was it for this, so many and so many
Have hackt their spirit-swords against our fetters
And killing cords, that bleed our hearts to death—
Wept griefs might turn the soul grey in an hour—
Broke their great hearts for love, and, in despair,
Dasht their immortal crowns to earth, and died?
Was it for this the countless Host of Martyrs,
Becrown'd and robed in fiery martyrdom,
Beat out a golden-aged Future from
The angel-metal of their noble lives—
Clomb the red scaffold—strain'd their weary eyes,
Across the mists of ages, for one glimpse
Of midnight burning into that bright Dawn
Now bursting golden, up the skies of time?
When will ye put your human glory on?
How long will ye lie darkling desolate,

With barren brain, blind life, and fallow heart ?
The hollow yearning grave will kindly close,
And flowers spring where the mould lay freshly dark !
The leaves will burst from out the naked'st boughs,
Fire-ripen'd into glorious greenery,
Waste Moor and Fen will kindle into spring ;
How long will ye lie darkling, desolate ?
Lord God Almighty ! what a spring of freedom
Awaits to burst the winter of our world !
O! if aught moving thrills a brother's love,
Which pleads for utterance in blinding tears,
Then let these words burn living in your souls,
Snatch Fear's cold hand from off your palsied hearts,
And send the intrepid shudder through your veins.
Helots of Albion ! Penury's nurslings ! rise,
And swear, in God's name, and in Heaven's or Hell's,
Ye will bear witness at the birth of Freedom !
Arise, and front the blessed light of Heaven,
With tyrant-quailing manhood in your looks !
Arise, go forth to glorious war for right,
And justice, and mankind's high destiny !
Arise, 'tis Freedom's bleeding fight, strike home
Wherever tyrants lift the gorgon-head !
There is a chasm in the coming years,
A-gape for strife's Niagara of blood—
Or to be bridged by brave hearts linkt in love.
The world is stirring with its mighty purpose :
No more be laggards in the march of men.

The Vulture Despotism spreads its wide wings
Right royally, to give ye broader mark !
And the hag Evil sickens unto death,
With her sore travail o'er the birth of God.
And yet shall War's red-letter'd creed die out :
Where blood is running, shall the wild-flowers blow ;
Where men are groaning, shall their children sing ;
And peace and love re-Genesis the world.

---

## EDEN.

THERE is not a rift in the blue sky now,
  Where a million tempests tore it ;
There is not a furrow on Ocean's brow,
  Tho' a million years have past o'er it.
And for all the storms and the strifes that have roll'd
  Down the ages grim and gory ;
Earth weareth her pleasant face, as of old,
  And laughs in her morning glory.
And Man—tho' he beareth the brand of Sin,
  And the flesh and the devil have bound him—
Hath a spirit within, to old Eden akin,
  Only nurture up Eden around him.

O the cloud may have fall'n on the human face,
  And its lordliest beauty blighted ;
For love hath gone out with a dark'ning trace,
  Where the inward glory lighted.
Yet the old world of love liveth still in the heart,
  As we've many a sweet revealing :
And its rich fossil-jewels in tears will up-start
  With the warm flood of holier feeling.
Ay, Man—tho' he beareth the brand of Sin,
  And the flesh and the devil have bound him—
Hath a spirit within, to old Eden akin,
  Only nurture up Eden around him

O tne terrors, the tortures, the miseries dark—
  That have curst us, and crusht, and cankered !
Yet, aye, from the Deluge, Humanity's Ark
  Hath on some serene Ararat anchored.
O the golden chains that link heaven to earth,
  The rusts of all time cannot sever !
Evil shall die in its own dark dearth,
  And the Good liveth on for ever.
And Man—tho' he beareth the brand of Sin,
  And the flesh and the devil have bound him—
Hath a spirit within, to old Eden akin,
  Only nurture up Eden around him.

## THE MEN OF FORTY-EIGHT.

THEY rose in Freedom's rare sunrise,
  Like Giants roused from wine ;
And in their hearts and in their eyes,
  The God leapt up divine !
Their souls flasht out like naked swords,
  Unsheathed for fiery fate !
Strength went like battle with their words—
  The Men of Forty-eight,
                    Hurrah !
  For the Men of Forty-eight.

Dark days have fall'n, yet in the strife
  They bate no hope sublime,
And bravely works the exultant life,
  Their hearts pulse thro' the time :
As grass is greenest trodden down,
  So suffering makes men great,
And this dark tide shall richly crown
  The work of Forty-eight,
                    Hurrah !
  For the Men of Forty-eight.

Some in a bloody burial sleep,
  Like Greeks to glory gone,
But in their steps avengers leap
  With their proof-armour on :
And hearts beat high with dauntless trust
  To triumph soon or late,
Tho' they be mould'ring down in dust—
  Brave Men of Forty-eight !
                Hurrah !
  For the Men of Forty-eight !

O when the world wakes up to worst
  The Tyrants once again,
And Freedom's summons-shout shall burst,
  Rare music ! on the brain,—
With heart to heart, in many a land,
  Ye'll find them all elate—
Brave remnant of that Spartan-band,
  The Men of Forty-eight.
                Hurrah !
  For the Men of Forty-eight.

## OUR LAND.

'Tis the Land that our stalwart fore-sires trode,
Where the brave and the heroic-soul'd
Implanted our freedom with their best blood,
In the martyr-days of old.
The huts of the lowly gave Liberty birth,
Their hearts were her cradle glorious,
And wherever her foot-prints lettered the earth,
Great spirits up-sprang victorious,
In our rare old Land, our dear old Land,
With its memories bright and brave,
And sing hey for the hour its sons shall band
To free it of Tyrant and Slave.

Alfred was of us, and Shakespeare's thought
Bekings us, all crowns above !
And Freedom's dear faith a fierce splendour caught
From our grand old Milton's love !
And we should be marching on gallantly,
And striding from glory to glory,
For the Right with our Might striking valiantly,
On the track of the famous in story—
For our rare old Land, our dear old Land,
With its memories bright and brave,

And sing hey for the hour its sons shall band
To free it of Tyrant and Slave.

On Naseby-field of the fight sublime,
Our old red Rose doth blow !
Would to God that the soul of that earlier time
Might marshal us conquering now !
On into the Future's fair clime the world sweeps,
And the time trumpets true men to freedom :
At the heart of our helots the mounting God leaps,
But O for the Moses to lead 'em !
For our rare old Land, our dear old Land,
With its memories bright and brave !
And sing hey for the hour its sons shall band
To free it of Tyrant and Slave.

What do we lack, that the ruffian Wrong
Should starve us 'mid heaps of gold ?
We have brains as broad, we have arms as strong,
We have hearts as big and as bold !
Will a thousand years more of meek suffering school
Our lives to a sterner bravery ?
No ! down and down with their robber rule,
And up from the land of slavery !
For our rare old Land, our dear old Land,
With its memories bright and brave !
And sing hey for the hour its sons shall band
To free it of Tyrant and Slave

## SWEET SPIRIT OF MY LOVE.

Sweet Spirit of my love !
Thro' all the world we walk apart :
Thou mayst not in my bosom lie :
I may not press thee to my heart,
Nor see love-thinkings light thine eye :
Yet art thou with me. All my life
Orbs out in thy warm beauty's sphere ;
My bravest dreams of thee are rife,
And coloured with thy presence dear.

Sweet Spirit of my love !
I know how beautiful thou art,
But never tell the starry thought :
I only whisper to my heart,
" She lights with heaven thy earthliest spot."
And birds that night and day rejoice,
And fragrant winds, give back to me
A music ringing of thy voice,
And surge my heart's love-tide to thee.

Sweet Spirit of my love !
The Spring and Summer bloom-bedight,
That garland Earth with rainbow-showers,—
Morn's kissing breath, and eyes of light,
That wake in smiles the winking flowers,
The air with honey'd fragrance fed,
The flashing waters,—soughing tree,—
Noon's golden glory,—sundown red,
Aye warble into songs of thee.

Sweet Spirit of my love !
When Night's soft silence clothes the earth,
And wakes the passionate bird of love ;
And Stars laugh out in golden mirth,
And yearning souls divinelier move ;
When God's breath hallows every spot,
And, lapp'd in feeling's luxury,
The heart's break-full of tender thought ;
Then art thou with me, still with me.

Sweet Spirit of my love !
I listen for thy footfall,—feel
Thy look is burning on me, such
As reads my heart : I sometimes reel
And throb, expectant for thy touch !

For by the voice of woods and brooks,
    And flowers with virgin-fragrance wet,
And earnest Stars with yearning looks,
    I know that we shall mingle yet.

Sweet Spirit of my love!
Strange places on me smile, as thou
    Hadst pass'd, and left thy beauty's tints:
The wild-flowers even the secret know,
    And light and shade flash mystic hints:
Meseems, like olden Gods, thou'lt come
    In cloud; but mine anointed eyes
Shall see the glory burn thro' gloom,
    And clasp thee, Sweet! with large surprise.

---

## THE BRIDAL.

She comes! the blushing Bridal Dawn,
With her Auroral splendours on!
And green Earth never lovelier shone:

She danceth on her golden way,
In dainty dalliance with the May,
Jubilant o'er the happy day!

Earth weareth heaven for bridal-ring,
And the best garland of glory, Spring
From out old Winter's world can bring.

The green blood reddens in the rose :
And underneath white-budding boughs
The violets purple in rich rows.

High up in air the Chestnuts blow,
The live-green Apple-tree's flush bough
Floateth, a cloud of rosy snow !

Cloud-shadow-ships swim faerily
Over the greenery's sunny sea,
Whose warm tides ripple down the lea.

The Birds, a-brooding, strive to sing,
Feeling the life warm 'neath the wing :
Their love, too, burgeons with the Spring !

The winds that make the flowers blow,
Heavy with balm, breathe soft and low,
A budding warmth, an amorous glow !

They kiss like some endearing mouth,
More sweet than the Sabean South,
And balm the splendour's drooping drouth :

Such a delicious feel doth flood
The eyes, as laves the burning bud
When June-rains feed ambrosial blood.

O, merrily Life doth revel and reign
Light in heart, and blithe in brain ;
Running like wine in every vein.

Alive with eyes, the Village sees
The Bridal dawning from the trees,
And Housewives swarm i' the sun like Bees.

Silence sits i' the Belfry-Choir !
Up in the twinkling air the spire
Throbs, golden in the bickering fire.

The winking windows burn and blush
With colours rare as flow and flush
Thrò' summer sunsets bloom'd and hush.

But, enter : lordlier splendours brim,
Such mists of gold and purple swim,
And the light falls so rich and dim.

Even so doth Love Life's doors unbar,
Where all the hidden glories are,
That from the windows shone afar.

Love's lovely to the passers-by,
But they who love are region'd high
On th' hills of Bliss, with heaven nigh.

Sumptuous as Iris, when she swims
With rainbow-robe on dainty limbs,
The Bride's rare loveliness o'erbrims !

The gazers drink rich overflows,
Her cheek a livelier damask glows,
And on his arm she leans more close.

A drunken joy reels in his blood,
He wanders an enchanted wood,
He ranges realms of perfect good.

Dear God ! that he alone hath grace
To light such splendour in her face,
And win the blessing of embrace !

She wears her maiden modesty
With tearful grace toucht tenderly,
Yet with a ripe Expectancy !

Her virgin veil reveals a form,
Flowering from the bud so warm,
It needs must break the Cestus-charm.

Last night, with wedable, white arms,
And thoughts that throng'd with quaint alarms,
She trembled o'er her mirror'd charms,

Like Eve first-glassing her new life ;
And the Maid startled at the Wife,
Heart-pained with a sweet, warm strife.

The unknown sea moans on her shore
Of life : she hears the breakers roar ;
But, trusting Him, she'll fear no more ;

For, o'er the deep seas there is calm,
Full as the hush of all-heaven's psalm :
The golden goal,—the Victor's palm !

And at her heart Love sits and sings,
And broodeth warmth, begetting wings
Shall lift her life to higher things.

The Blessing given, the ring is on ;
And at God's Altar radiant run
The currents of two lives in one !

Husht with happiness, every sense
Is crowded at the heart intense ;
And silence hath such eloquence !

Down to his feet her meek eyes stoop,
As *there* her love should pour its cup ;
But, like a King, he lifts them up.

Her flashing face to heaven up-turns,
As for God's gracious kiss it yearns :
Through all her life Hope's sunrise burns !

And now she trembles to his breast,
To make it aye her happy nest,
And proudly crown his loving quest :

His arms her hyacinth head caress,
And fold her fragrant slenderness,
With all its touching tenderness.

Now, on heaven's coast of crystal crown'd
Hesper lights life's outward-bound :
And Evening folds her purple round.

A palace rich with glorious shows
She maketh his life's narrow house
To-night : but there he keeps no rouse !

Alone they hold their marriage-feast :
Fresh from the Chrism of the Priest,
He would not have the happiest jest

To storm her brows with a crimson fine ;
And, sooth, they need no wings of wine
To waft them into Love's divine.

So Strength and Beauty, hand-in-hand,
Go forth into the honey'd land,
Lit by the love-moon golden-grand,

Where God hath built their Bridal-bower ;
And on the top of life they tower,
And taste of Eden's perfect hour.

No lewd eyes o'er my shoulder look !
They do but ope the blessed book
Of Marriage in their hallowed nook.

O, flowery be the paths they press,
And ruddiest human fruitage bless
Them, with a lavish loveliness !

Melodious move their wedded life
Thro' shocks of time, and storms of strife,—
Husband true, and perfect Wife !

## A GLIMPSE OF AULD LANG-SYNE.

Earth, garnisht Bride-like, bares her bosom to the nestling Night,
Who hath come down in glory from the golden halls of light.

Ten thousand tender, starry eyes smile o'er the world at rest,
The weary world—husht like an infant on its mother's breast!

The great old hills thrust up their foreheads in rich-sleeping light:
How proudly-grand, and still they stand, worshipping God to-night!

The flowers have hung their cups with gems of their own sweetness wrought,
And muse upon their stems, in smiling ecstasy of thought:

They have banquetted on beauty, at the fragrant Eve's red lips,
And fold in charmed rest, with crowns upon their velvet tips.

No green tide sweeps the sea of leaves, no wind-sigh stirs
the sod,
While Holiness broods dove-like on the soul, begetting
God.

Sweet hour ! thou wak'st the feeling that we never know
by day,
For Angel eyes look down, and read the spirit 'neath the
clay :

Even while I list, such music stealeth in upon my soul,
As though adown heaven's stair of stars, the seraph-
harpings stole—

Or I could grasp the immortal part of life, and soar, and
soar,
Such strong wings take me, and my heart hath found such
hidden lore !

It flings aside the weight of years, and lovingly goes back,
To that sweet time, the dear old time, that glistens on its
track !

Life's withered leaves grow green again, and fresh with
Childhood's spring,
As I am welcomed back once more, within its rainbow-
ring :—

The Past, with all its gather'd charms, beckons me back
in joy,
And loving hearts, and open arms, re-clasp me as a boy.

The voices of the Loved and Lost are stirring at my
heart,
And Memory's miser'd treasures lead to life, with sudden
start,—

As, through her darkened windows, warm and glad sun-
light creeps in,
And Lang-syne, glimpst in glorious tears, my toil-worn
heart doth win.

Thou art looking, smiling on me, as thou hast lookt and
smiled, Mother,
And I am sitting by thy side, at heart a very child,
Mother!

I'm with thee now in soul, sweet Mother, much as in
those hours,
When all my wealth was in thy love, and in the birds and
flowers,

When the long summer days were short, for my glad soul
to live
The golden fulness of the bliss, each happy hour could
give.

When Heaven sang to my innocence, and every leafy grove
And forest ach'd with music, as a young heart aches with love.

When life oped like a flower, where clung my lips, to quaff its honey,
And joys throng'd like a shower of gold king-cups in meadows sunny.

I'll tell thee, Mother! since we met, stern changes have come o'er me:
Then life smiled like a paradise, the world was all before me.

O! I was full of trustful faith and, in my glee and gladness,
Deemed not that others had begun as bright, whose end was madness.

I knew not smiles could light up eyes, like Sunset's laughing glow
On some cold stream, which burns above, while all runs dark below;

That on Love's summer sea, great souls go down, while some, grown cold,
Seal up Affection's living spring, and sell their love for gold;

How they on whom we'd staked the heart forget the early
vow,
And they who swore to love through life would pass all
coldly now ;

How, in the soul's dark hour, Love's temple-veil is rent
in twain,
And the heart quivers thorn-crown'd on the cross of fiery
pain.

And shatter'd idols, broken dreams, come crowding on
my brain,
As speaks the spirit-voice of days that never come again

It tells of golden moments lost—heart seared—blind Pas-
sion's thrall ;
Life's spring-tide blossoms run to waste, Love's honey
turn'd to gall.

It tells how many and often high resolve and purpose
strong,
Shaped on the anvil of my heart, have died upon my
tongue.

I left thee, mother, in sweet May, the merry month of
flowers,
To toil away in dusky gloom the golden summer-hours.

I left my world of love behind, with soul for life a-thirsting;
My burning eyelid dropt no tear, although my heart was bursting.

For I had knit my soul to climb, with poverty its burden;
Give me but time, O give me time, and I would win the guerdon.

Ah, Mother! many a heart that all my aspiration cherisht
Hath fallen in the trampling strife, and in the life-march perisht.

We see the bleeding victims lie upon the world's grim Altar,
And one by one young feelings die, and dark doubts make us falter.

Mother, the world hath wreakt its part on me, with scathing power,
Yet the best life that heaves my heart runs for thee at this hour,

And by these holy yearnings, by these eyes with sweet tears wet,
I know there wells a spring of love through all my being yet.

## SONG OF THE RED REPJBLICAN.

Fling out the red Banner ! its fiery front under,
Come, gather ye, gather ye, Champions of Right !
And roll round the world, with the voice of God's thunder,
The Wrongs we've to reckon, oppressions to smite,
They deem that we strike no more like the old Hero-band,
Victory's own battle-hearted and brave :
Blood of Christ ! brothers mine, it were sweet but to see ye stand,
Triumph or Tomb welcome, Glory or Grave !

Fling out the red Banner in mountain and valley !
Let Earth feel the tread of the free once again ;
Now soldiers of Freedom, for love of God, rally,
Old Earth yearns to know that her children are Men.
We are nerved by a thousand wrongs, burning and bleeding ;
Bold Thoughts leap to birth, but the bold Deeds must come ;
And wherever Humanity's yearning and pleading,
One battle for Liberty strike we heart-home.

Fling out the red Banner ! achievements immortal
  Have yet to be won by the hands labour-brown ;
And few, few may enter the proud promise-portal,
  Yet were it in thought like a glorious Crown !
And O joy of the onset ! sound trumpet, array us ;
  True hearts would leap up were all hell in our path.
Up, up from the Slave-land ; who stirreth to stay us,
  Shall fall, as of old, in the Red Sea of wrath.

Fling out the red Banner, O Sons of the morning !
  Young spirits abiding to burst into wings,—
We stand shadow-crown'd, but sublime is the warning,
  All heaven's grimly husht, and the Bird of Storm
    sings !
" All's well," saith the Sentry on Tyranny's tower,
  While Hope by his watch-fire is grey and tear-blind ;
Ay, all's well ! Freedom's Altar burns, hour by hour,
  Live brands for the fire-damp with which ye are mined.

Fling out the red Banner ! the patriots perish,
  But where their bones whiten the seed striketh root :
Their blood hath run red the great harvest to cherish :
  Then gather ye, Reapers, and garner the fruit.
Victory ! victory ! Tyrants are quaking !
  The Titan of Toil from the bloody thrall starts ;
The slaves are awaking, the dawn-light is breaking,
  The foot-fall of Freedom beats quick at our hearts !

## THE PATRIOT TO HIS BRIDE.

Will you leave the fond bosom of Home, where
  Bliss hath been from your earliest waking?
Can you give its endearments to come, where
  Life hath many a hot heart-aching?
Have you counted the cost to stand by me,
  In the battle I fight for Man?
And shall your angel-love deify me,
  Who stand in the world's dark ban?
O, a daring high soul you will need, dear love,
  To brave the life-battle with me:
For your true heart may oftentimes bleed, dear love,
  And your sweet eyes dim tearfully.

Sweet! know you of gallant hearts perishing,—
  The fine spirits that dumbly bow?
For a little of Fortune's cherishing,
  They are breaking in agony now!
And without the sunshine that life needeth,
  Alas! Sweet! for me and for you:
But little the careless world heedeth
  For love like ours, tender and true!

O, a daring high soul you will need, dear love,
  To brave the life-battle with me :
For your true heart may oftentimes bleed, dear love,
  And your sweet eyes dim tearfully.

Well, you've sworn, I have sworn, God hath bound us,
  In a covenant the world shall not part;
I have flung my love's purple around us,
  And you live in each pulse of my heart!
It may be our name in Earth's story
  Shall endure when we are no more ;
For love lives as the Stars burn in glory,
  And the Flowers bud on Earth's green floor.
But a daring high soul you will need, dear love,
  To brave the life-battle with me :
For your true heart may oftentimes bleed, dear love,
  And your sweet eyes dim tearfully.

---

## ANATHEMA MARANATHA.

Deeper and deeper the Tyrant's lash flayeth,
Swifter and swifter grim Misery slayeth ;
Tighter and tighter the grip of Toil groweth,
Nearer and nearer the dark Ruin floweth.

And still ye bear on, and ye faint heart and breath,
Till ye creep, scourgéd hounds, to your kennel of death:
O down to the dust with ye, cowards and slaves,
Plague-stricken cumber-grounds, slink to your graves!

Love is the crown of all life, but ye wear it not;
Freedom, Humanity's palm, and ye bear it not;
Beauty spreads banquet for all, but ye share it not;
Grimmer the blinding veil glooms, and ye tear it not.
Weaving your life flowers in Wrong's robe of glory,
Ye stint in your starkness with hearts smitten hoary:
O down to the dust with ye, cowards and slaves,
Plague-stricken cumber-grounds, slink to your graves!

They have broken our hearts for their hunger, and trod
The wine-press for Death, with the grapes of our God;
And ye lick their feet, red with your blood, like dumb
cattle:
Ah! better and braver to meet them in battle!
The bow that Tell drew hath lost none of its spring,
But ye nerve not with daring the arrow and string:
Then down to the dust with ye, cowards and slaves,
Plague-stricken cumber-grounds, slink to your graves!

There's a curse on the Mammonites fiery and fell,
Gold turns their hard hearts into hearthstones for hell;
And there's wringing of hands with the Knave and the
Tyrant,
For God's graven autograph's on their death-warrant,

While lordlier manhood 'neath Freedom's heart yearneth,
Up now ! while before ye the fire-pillar burneth !
Or down to the dust with ye, cowards and slaves,
Down, down for ever, and slink to your graves !

---

## THE LORDS OF LAND AND MONEY.

Sons of Old England, from the sod,
Up-lift the noble brow !
Gold apes a mightier power than God,
And wealth is worshipt now !
In all these toil-ennobled lands
Ye have no heritage :
They snatch the fruit of youthful hands,
The staff from weary age.
O tell them in their Palaces,
These lords of Land and Money !
They shall not kill the poor like bees,
To rob them of Life's honey.

Thro' long dark years of blood and tears,
We've toil'd like branded slaves,
Till Wrong's red hand hath made a land
Of paupers, prisons, graves !

But our long-sufferance endeth now,
  Within the souls of men
The fruitful buds of promise blow,
  And Freedom lives again!
O tell them in their Palaces,
  These Lords of Land and Money!
They shall not kill the poor like bees,
  To rob them of Life's honey.

Too long have Labour's nobles knelt
  Before exalted "Rank;"
Within our souls the iron is felt—
  We hear our fetters clank!
A glorious voice goes throbbing forth
  From millions stirring now,
Who yet before these Gods of earth
  Shall stand with unblencht brow.
O tell them in their Palaces,
  These Lords of Land and Money!
They shall not kill the poor like bees,
  To rob them of Life's honey.

## LITTLE LILYBELL.

WHEN unseen fingers part the leaves,
And show us Beauty's face ;
And Earth her breast of glory heaves
And glows from Spring's embrace :
When Flowers on green and golden wings
Float up—Life's sea cloth swell
And flush a world of vernal things,—
Came little Lilybell.

And like a blessed Bird of calm
Our love's sweet wants she stilled,
Made Passion's fiery wine run balm,—
Life's glory half fulfilled !
From dappled dawn to twinkling dark,
This witching Ariel
Fills all our heaven : or like a Lark
Sings little Lilybell.

And she is fair, O very fair,—
Has eyes so like the dove !
And lightly leans her world of care
Upon our arms of love !

It cannot be that ye will break
  The promise-tale ye tell,
Ye will not make such fond hearts ache,
  O little Lilybell !

As on Life's stream her leaflets spread,
  And tremble in its flow,
We shudder, lest the awful Dead
  Pluck at her from below !
Breathe softly low, ye Winds that start,—
  O stream, but faintly swell :
Your every motion smites the heart,
  For little Lilybell.

We tremble : lest the angel Death,
  Who comes to gather flowers
For Paradise—at her sweet breath,
  Should fall in love with ours !
O many a year may come and go
  Ere from Life's mystic well
Such stream shall flow—such flower shall blow,
  As our sweet Lilybell.

Oh ! when thy dear heart fills with fears,
  And aches with Love's sweet pain,
And pale cheeks burn thro' happy tears
  Like red Rose in the rain—

I marvel Sweet! if we shall see
  The sight and say 'tis well,
When the Beloved calls for thee,
  Our dainty Lilybell?

How rich Love made the lowly sod
  Where such a Flower hath blown!
O Love, we love, and think that God
  Is such a love full-grown!
Dear God, that gave the blessed trust,
  Be near, that all be well,
And morn and eve bedew our dust,
  For love of Lilybell.

---

## THE GOLDEN WEDDING-RING.

With a white hand like a lady,
  And a heart as merry as Spring,
I am ripe and I am ready
  For a golden wedding-ring.

As the earth with sea is bounded,
  And the Winter-world with Spring,
So a Maiden's life is rounded
  With a golden wedding-ring.

This old world is scarce worth seeing,
  Till Love waves his purple wing,
And we gauge the bliss of being,
  Thro' a golden wedding-rimg.

Would you draw far Edens nearer
  And to Earth the angels bring,
You must seek the magic mirror
  Of a golden wedding-ring.

I have known full many a Maiden
  Like a white Rose withering,
Into fresh ripe beauty redden
  Thro' a golden wedding-ring.

Fainting spirits oft grow fearless,
  Sighing hearts will soar and sing,
Tearful eyes will laugh out tearless,
  Thro' a golden wedding-ring.

There's no jewel so worth wearing,
  That a Lover's hands may bring,
There's no treasure worth comparing
  With a golden wedding-ring.

As the crescent Moon rings golden
  Her full beauty perfecting,
Woman's glory is unfolden
  In a golden wedding-ring.

Ah ! when hearts are wildly beating,
  And when arms all glowing cling,
Think Love's circle wants completing
  With a golden wedding-ring.

---

## THE UNBELOVED.

Like a tree beside the river
  Of her life that runs from me,
Do I lean me, murmuring ever
  My fond love's idolatry :
And I reach out hands of blessing,
  And I stretch out hands of prayer,
And with passionate caressing,
  Waste my life upon the air.
In my ears the Syren river
  Sings, and smiles up in my face ;
But for ever and for ever
  Runs from my embrace.

Spring by spring, the branches duly
  Clothe themselves in tender Flower,
And for her sweet sake as truly
  All their fruit and fragrance shower ;

But, the stream with careless laughter,
  Runs in merry beauty by,
And it leaves me yearning after—.
  Lone to weep, and lone to die !
In my ears the Syren river
  Sings, and smiles up in my face ;
But, for ever and for ever,
  Runs from my embrace.

I stand 'mazèd in the moonlight,
  O'er its happy face to dream !
I am parchèd in the noonlight,
  By that cool and brimming stream !
I am dying by the river
  Of her life that runs from me !
While it sparkles by me ever
  With its cool felicity !
In my ears the Syren river
  Sings, and smiles up in my face ;
But, for ever and for ever,
  Runs from my embrace.

## DESERTED.

Love came to me in a rosy cloud,
  With a golden glory kist ;
And caught me up, and in heaven we rode,
  Till it melted in mournful mist.
Gone ! gone ! is the light that shone,
  With the dream of my earlier day :
And the wild winds moan, and alone, alone,
  I wander my weary way.

The days come and go, and the seasons roll,—
  In their glory they pass me by ;
And the lords of life and the happy in soul
  Walk under a smiling sky.
And the sweet springtide comes back to earth, o'er
  The soothèd winter sea ;
But He will return no more, no more,
  Never come back to me.

It were better that I lay sleeping
  With his baby upon my breast,
When the weary have done with their weeping
  And the wretched are rockt to their rest.

The world is a desolate, dreary one,
  And full of sad tears at best:
God, take back thy wandering weary one,
  Like a wounded bird home to its nest.

---

## LOVE IN IDLENESS.

We sit serenely 'neath the Night,
As still as stars, with swift delight;
In tears, that tell how in Life's deep
The hidden pearls of beauty sleep;
And silent, as of sleeping Seas,
And quiet, as of dreaming Trees:
The river of our bliss runs filled,
Its faintest happy murmur stilled.

Upon my forehead rests thy palm,
And on my spirit rests thy calm:
I cannot see thy face, but know
Its sea of rose-bloom hath a glow
Like ruby light: and richly lies
The dew and shadows in thine eyes;
That ask how they may soothliest bless,
Like crystal-wells of tenderness.

Warm fragrance, like the soul o' the South,
Is round thee ; and thy damask mouth
Dissolves me in delicious death,
It doth so breathe ambrosial breath !
Musk-roses blowing in the gloom,
Drop fragrance fainting in the room ;
And such fine sadness fills the air,
Ripe Life a bloom of dew doth wear.

We sit, with silent glory crowned,
And Love's arms wound in amorous round ;
As on rich clouds of fragrance swim
The summer dusk, so cool, and dim !
While we our fields of pleasure reap
Our Babes lie in the wood of Sleep ;
One—first love's dream of beauty wrought !
One—the more perfect after-thought !

The harping hand hath dulled the lyre
Of thrilling heart-strings. By their fire
Droopt low, the dreamy Passions doze,
In large luxuriance of repose.
I only see—that thou art near ;
I only feel—I have thee, Dear !
I only hear thy throbbing heart,
And know that we can never part.

## DOWN IN AUSTRALIA.

QUAFF a cup, and send a cheer up for the Old Land!
We have heard the Reapers shout,
For the Harvest going out,
With the smoke of battle closing round the bold Land:
And our message shall be hurled
Up the ringing sides o' the world,
There are true hearts beating for you in the Gold Land.

We are with you in your battles, brave and bold Land!
For the old ancestral tree
Striketh root beneath the sea,
And it beareth fruit of Freedom in the Gold Land!
We shall come too, if you call,
We shall fight on if you fall,
Cromwell's land must never be a bought and sold Land.

O the standard of the Lord wave o'er the Old Land!
For, the waiting world holds breath
While she treads the dew of Death,
With the sleeve of Peace stript up from her bare, bold hand:

And her ruddy Rose will bloom
On the bosom and the tomb
Of her many Heroes fallen for the Old Land.

O, a terror to the Tyrant is the Old Land!
He remembers how she stood
With her raiment rolled in blood,
When the tide of battle burst upon the bold Land,
And he looks with darkened face,
For he knows the hero-race
Sweep the harp of Freedom—draw her Sword with bold hand.

Let thy glorious voice be heard thou great and bold Land!
Speak the one victorious word,
And fair Freedom's wandered Bird
Shall wing back with leaf of promise from the Old Land!
And the Peoples shall come out
From their slavery, with a shout
For the new world greeting in the Future's Gold Land.

When the smoke of Battle rises from the Old Land,
You shall see the Tyrant down,
You shall see the ransomed crown,
On the brow of prisoned peoples, freed with bold hand!
She shall thrash her foes like corn;
They shall eat the bread of scorn,
And will sing her song of Triumph in the Gold Land.

Quaff a cup, and send a cheer up from the Gold Land,
We have heard the Reapers shout,
For the harvest going out,
Seen the smoke of battle closing round the bold Land,
And our message shall be hurled
Up the ringing sides o' the world,
There are true hearts down here, beating for the Old
Land

---

## THE EXILE TO HIS COUNTRY.

How dimmed is all thy glory, and how dark the shadow
falls !
And wild the sorrow waileth thro' thy hamlets and thy
halls !
Thy banner burns no longer on the mountains and the sea,
And oh ! the dead are blessed who thy suffering may not
see.
How are thy brave ones scattered on many an alien
strand !
Thy darlings leal and true to the dear old Motherland.

They have bound thee in the grave-clothes, but, we watch
with tears and sighs,
Till Freedom comes like Christ, and thou like Lazarus
shalt rise.

Thy pale, pale face, my Country, yet shall flush with ripen-
ing bloom,
As Nature's color kindles when the breath of Spring doth
come.
Oh! come thou Spring of promise; mighty Hope, put forth
thy hand,
And build thy arch of triumph for the dear old Mother-
land.

The Birds that follow Summer, they come and they depart,
For the Land of my love, and the home of my heart:
And, like a wounded Bird, my spirit trembles in the wind,
And flutters down: and they are gone and I am left
behind!
O my Dovelets in the net! O the spoiler's bloody hand!
And I so far away from the dear old Motherland.

Sometimes when life is darkest, a glory bursts its glooms,
As Lightning thro' the startled night, the face of things
illumes;
A sudden splendour smites me, and ere the thunders roll,
I see thy face look radiant thro' the darkness of my soul!
And thou art sitting at the feet of Freedom, great and
grand,
Thy children happy in thy smile, thou dear old Mother-
land.

O thou among the nations, for thy might shalt yet be themed,
Thy fatal curse of Beauty by Love's blessing all redeemed!
The red wounds where they pierced thee, shall to scars of glory turn,
And in thy tearful eyes the light of boundless life shall burn!
The heavens are filled with Martyrs, but the earth still holds a band
Who meet in battle yet for the dear old Motherland.

Oh! many are the gallant hearts will never answer when
Thy clarion-cry shall call us up to the field again!
And many are the tears must fall, and prayers go up to God,
But swift the vintage ripens, and the winepress shall be trod!
The Harvest reddens rich for death! the Reapers clench the hand,
And Victory comes to wed his bride, thou dear old Motherland.

## THE DESERTER FROM THE CAUSE.

He is gone: better so. We should know who stand
under
Our Banner: let none but the trusty remain!
For there's stern work at hand, and the time comes shall
sunder
The shell from the pearl, and the chaff from the grain!
And the heart that thro' danger and death will be dutiful—
Soul that with Cranmer in fire would shake hands;
With a Life, like a palace-home built for the Beautiful;
Freedom of all her Beloved demands!

He is gone from us! Yet shall we march on victorious,
Hearts burning like Beacons—eyes fixt on the Goal!
And if we fall fighting, we fall like the Glorious;
With face to the Stars, and all heaven in the soul!
And aye for the brave stir of battle we'll barter
The sword of life sheatht in the peace of the grave:
And better the fieriest fate of the Martyr,
Than live like the Coward, and die like the Slave!

## THEY ARE BUT GIANTS WHILE WE KNEEL.

Good People ! put no faith in Kings, nor in your Princes
trust,
Who break your hearts for bread, and grind your faces in
the dust !
The Palace Paupers look from lattice high and mock your
prayer :
The Champions of the Christ are dumb, or golden bit they
wear !
O but to see ye bend no more to earth's crime-curséd
things—
Ye are God's Oracles : stand forth ! be Nature's Priests
and Kings !
Ye fight and bleed, while Fortune's darlings slink in
splendid lair ;
With lives that crawl, like worms through buried Beauty's
golden hair !—
A tale of lives wrung out in tears their Grandeur's garb
reveals,
And the last sobs of breaking hearts sound in their Cha-
riot-wheels !

O league ye—crush the things that kill all love and liberty !
They are but Giants while we kneel : ONE LEAP, AND UP GO WE.

Trust not the Priests, their tears are lies, their hearts are hard and cold ;
They lead ye to sweet pastures, where they fleece the foolish fold !
The Church and State are linkt and sworn to desolate the land.
Good people, 'twixt these Foxes' tails, We'll fling a fiery brand !
Up, if ye will be free, to golden calves no longer bow :
The Nations yearn for liberty—the world is earnest now !
Your bent-knee is half-way to hell !—Up, Serviles, from the dust !
The Harvest of the free red-ripens for the sickle-thrust.
They're quaking now, and shaking now, who've wrought the hurtling sorrow,
To-day the desolators, but the desolate To-morrow !
Loud o'er their murder's menace wakes the watchword of the Free :
They are but Giants while we kneel ; ONE LEAP, AND UP GO WE !

Some bravest patriot-hearts have gone, to break beyond the Sea.
And many in the dungeon have died for you and me!
And still we glut the Merciless—give all Life's glory up,
That stars of flame, and winking eyes, may crown their revel-cup!
Back, tramplers on the Many! Death and Danger ambusht lie;
Beware ye, or the blood may run! the patient people cry;
Ah! shut not out the light of hope, or we may blindly dash.
Like Samson in his strong death-grope, and whelm ye in the crash;
Think how they spurned the People mad, that old Régime of France,
Whose heads like poppies from Death's Scythe fell in a bloody dance.
Ye plead in vain, ye bleed in vain, ah! Blind! when will ye see
They are but Giants while we kneel? ONE LEAP, AND UP GO WE.

The merry flowers are springing from our last-year Martyrs' mould,
As their dreams had taken blossom telling what they would have told;

Of all our rainbowed Future ; and what this earth shall be,
When we have bartered blows and bonds for life and liberty.
Ah ! what a face of glory shall the weary world put on,
When Love is crownéd, and shall king the heart its royal throne !
O we shall see our darlings smile,—who meet us tearful now,—
Ere the Eternal morn breaks grey, on the Beloved's brow :
And Love shall give the kiss of Death no more to those we love,
And pride, not shame, shall flush the face of our heart-nestling Dove.
Rouse, Titans, scale th' Olympus where the hindering Tyrants be :
They are but Giants while we kneel ; ONE LEAP, AND UP GO WE.

## THE CRY OF THE UNEMPLOYED.

'Tis hard, 'tis hard to wander on through this bright world of ours,
Beneath a sky of smiling blue, on velvet paths of flowers,
With music in the woods, as there were nought but joyance known,
Or Angels walkt earth's solitudes, and yet with want to groan,
To see no beauty in the stars, nor in God's radiant smile,
To wail and wander misery-curst! willing, but cannot toil.
There's burning sickness at my heart, I sink down famishéd!
God of the wretched, hear my prayer: I would that I were dead!

Heaven dropped down with manna still in many a golden show'r,
And feeds the leaves with fragrant breath, with silver dew the flow'r.
There's honeyed fruit for bee and bird, with bloom laughs out the tree,
And food for all God's happy things; but none gives food to me.

Earth, deckt with Plenty's garland-crown, smiles on my
aching eye,
The purse-proud,—swathed in luxury—disdainful pass
me by ;
I've eager hands, and earnest heart—but may not work
for bread !
God of the wretched, hear my prayer : I would that I were
dead !

Gold, art thou not a blessed thing : a charm above all
other,
To shut up hearts to Nature's cry, when brother pleads
with brother ?
Hast thou a music sweeter than the voice of loving-
kindness ?
No ! curse thee, thou'rt a mist 'twixt God and man in
outer blindness.
" Father, come back !" my children cry ; their voices,
once so sweet,
Now quiver lance-like in my bleeding heart ! I cannot
meet
The looks that make the brain go mad, for dear ones
asking bread—
God of the wretched, hear my prayer : I would that I were
dead !

Lord ! what right have the poor to wed ? Love's for the gilded great :
Are they not form'd of nobler clay, who dine off golden plate ?
'Tis the worst curse of Poverty to have a feeling heart :
Why can I not, with iron-grasp, tear out the tender part ?
I cannot slave in yon Bastille ! ah no 't were bitterer pain,
To wear the Pauper's iron within, than drag the Convict's chain.
I'd work but cannot, starve I may, but will not beg for bread :
God of the wretched, hear my prayer : I would that I were dead !

---

## I LOVE MY LOVE, AND MY LOVE LOVES ME.

THE life of life's when for another we're living,
Whose spirit responds to ours like a sweet Psalter ;
When heart-smiles are burning, and flame-words outgiving
The fire we have lit on her heart's holy Altar !
O Love, God's religion ! Love, burning and starried !
The soul must be beautiful where thou art palaced ;
I mark where thy kiss-seal is set on the forehead,

I know where thy dew of heaven's richliest chaliced.
That radiant brow breaketh thro' cloud and world-stain,
And strong is that soul in the battle of Duty ;
Smiling May-sunshine thro' Life's Winter-rain,
All outer things clothing with inner-world beauty !
'Tis writ in the face, whose heart singeth for glee,
"I love my Love, and my Love loves me."

Once I was a-weary of life and the world,
And the voice of Delight on my heart fell accurst,
And my eyes oft with tear-drops unweetingly pearl'd,
I had no one to love, tho' with love my heart burst :
Then on me a sweet dream of Paradise stole—
Turn'd to radiance the shadows that brooded around me ;
And walking the gardens that Eden my soul,
One morning, my Love, like another Eve, found me :
She lookt, and a maëlstrom of joy whirled my bosom ;
She smiled, and my being ran bliss to the brim :
She spake, and my eager heart flusht into blossom ;
Dear Heaven ! 'twas the music set to my Life's hymn !
And up went my soul to God, shouting for glee—
"I love my Love, and my Love loves me."

I know, Love of mine ! time may nevermore bring
Back the lost freshness that clad my young heart :
But, looking on thee, dear ! sweet thoughts will up-spring,
As from the cold tomb the green verdure will start !

I look in thine eyes, and, O joy to the weeper !
  Their love-light makes sunshine of all my dark fears ;
And what made my heart faint, lifts it now, a strong
    leaper !
  And rivers of bliss flood its channels of tears.
I had deem'd its wealth flung on sands barren and burning,
  And sweet 't is to find my Life's current again,
Caught up in thy Love's precious chalice—returning
  Like dew that hath been to heaven, dropping in rain.
    And my heart's perpetual hymn shall be,
    "I love my Love, and my Love loves me."

---

## THE THREE VOICES.

A WAILING voice comes up a desolate road,
      Drearily, drearily, drearily !
Where mankind have trodden the by-way of blood,
      Wearily, wearily, wearily !
Like a sound from the Dead Sea all shrouded in glooms,
  With breaking of hearts, fetters clanking, men groan-
    ing ;
Or chorus of Ravens, that croak among tombs,
  It comes with the mournfullest moaning :

"Weep, weep, weep!"
Yoke-fellows, listen,
Till tearful eyes glisten :
'T is the voice of the Past : the dark, grim-featured Past,
All sad as the shriek of the midnight blast :
Weep, weep, weep,
Tears to wash out the red, red stain,
Where earth hath been fatted
By brave hearts that rotted,
And life ran a deluge of hot, bloody rain :
Weep, weep, weep.

Another voice comes from the millions that bend,
Tearfully, tearfully, tearfully!
From hearts which the scourges of Slavery rend,
Fearfully, fearfully, fearfully!
From many a worn, noble spirit that breaks,
In the world's solemn shadows adown in Life's valleys,
From Mine, Forge, and Loom, trumpet-tongued it awakes,
On the soul wherein Liberty rallies :
"Work, work, work."
Yoke-fellows, listen,
Till earnest eyes glisten :
'T is the voice of the Present. It bids us, my brothers,
Be Freemen : and then for the freedom of others
Work, work, work!

For the Many a holocaust long to the Few :
O work while ye may !
O work while 't is day !
And cling to each other, united and true :
Work, work, work.

There cometh another voice sweetest of all,
Cheerily, cheerily, cheerily !
And my heart leapeth up at its glorious call,
Merrily, merrily, merrily !
It comes like the soft touch of Spring-tide, un-warping
The thrall of oppression that bound us :
It comes like a choir of the Seraphim, harping
Their gladsomest music around us :
" Hope, hope, hope !"
Yoke-fellows, listen,
Till gleeful eyes glisten :
'T is the voice of the Future, the sweetest of all,
That makes the heart leap to its glorious call.
Hope, hope, hope !
Brothers, step forth in the Future's van,
For the worst is past,
Right conquers at last,
And the better day dawns upon suffering man :
Hope, hope, hope.

## THE WORKER.

I care not a curse though from birth he inherit
  The tear-bitter bread and the stingings of scorn,
If the man be but one of God's nobles in spirit,—
  Though penniless, richly soul'd,—heartsome, though worn—
And will not for golden bribe lout it or flatter,
  But clings to the Right aye, as steel to the pole :
He may sweat at the plough, loom, or anvil, no matter,
  I'll own him the man that is dear to my soul.

His hand may be hard, and his raiment be tatter'd,
  On straw-pallet nightly his weary limbs rest ;
If his brow wear the stamp of a spirit unfetter'd,
  I'm mining at once for the gems in his breast.
Give me the true man, who will fear not nor falter,
  Though Want be his guerdon, the Workhouse his goal,
Till his heart has burnt out upon Liberty's Altar :
  For this is the man I hold dear to my soul.

True hearts, in this brave world of blessings and beauty.
  Aye scorn the poor splendour of losel and lurker ;
And Toil is creation's crown, worship is duty,
  And greater than Gods in old days is the Worker.

For us the wealth-laden world laboureth ever ;
  For us harvests ripen, winds blow, waters roll ;
And him who gives back in his might of endeavour,
  I'll cherish,—a man ever dear to my soul.

---

## THE AWAKENING OF THE PEOPLE.

O sweet is the fair face of Nature, when Spring
  With living flower-rainbow in glory hath spann'd
Hill and dale ; and the music of birds on the wing
  Makes earth seem a beautiful faëry land !
And dear is our first-love's young spirit-wed bride,
  With her meek eyes just sheathing in tender eclipse,
When the sound of our voice calls her heart's ruddy tide,
  Uprushing in beauty to melt on her lips.
But Earth has no sight half so glorious to see,
As a People up-girding its might to be free.

To see men awake from the slumber of ages,
  With brows grim from labour, and hands hard and tan,
Start up living heroes, the dreamt-of by Sages !
  And smite with strong arm the oppressors of man :

To see them come dauntless forth 'mid the world's warring,
Slaves of the midnight-mine ! serfs of the sod !
Show how the Eternal within them is stirring,
And never more bend to a crowned clod :
Dear God ! 'tis a sight for Immortals to see,—
A People up-girding its might to be free.

Battle on bravely, O sons of humanity !
Dash down the cup from your lips, O ye Toilers !
Too long hath the world bled for Tyrants' insanity—
Too long our weakness been strength to our spoilers.
For Freedom and Right, gallant hearts, wrestle ever,
And speak ye to others the proud word that won ye :
Your rights conquer'd once, shall be wrung from you never ;
O battle on bravely ; the world's eyes are on ye ;
And Earth hath no sight half so glorious to see,
As a People up-girding its might to be free !

---

## PRESS ON.

Press on, press on, ye Rulers, in the roused world's forward track :
It moves too sure for ye to put the clock of Freedom back !

We're gathering up from near and far, with souls in fiery glow,
And Right doth bare its arm of might, to bring the spoilers low,
Kings, Priests, ye're far too costly, and we weary of your rule ;
We crown no more "Divinity," where Nature writeth "Fool !"
Ye must not bar our glorious path as in the days agone ;
We know that God made Men, not Princes, Kings, or Priests.—Press on !

Press on, press on, ah ! "Nobles !" ye have play'd a daring game ;
But your star of strength is failing, fades the prestige of your name :
Too long have ye been fed and nurst on human blood and tears ;
The naked truth is known, and Labour leaps to life, and swears
His pride of strength to bloated Ease he will no longer give :
For all who live should labour ; "Lords," then all who work might live !
The combat comes ! make much of what ye've wrung from Fatherland !
Press on, press on ! To-day we plead, To-morrow we'll command.

Press on! a million pauper-foreheads bend in Misery's
dust;
God's champions of the golden Truth still eat the mouldy
crust:
This damning curse of Tyrants must not kill the nation's
heart;
The spirit in a million Slaves doth pant on fire to start,
And strive to mend the world, and walk in Freedom's
march sublime;
While myriads sink heart-broken, and the land o'er-
swarms with crime.
"O God!" they cry, "we die, we die, and see no earnest
won!"
Brothers, join hand and heart, and in the work press on,
press on!

---

## MERRY CHRISTMAS EVE.

MERRY Christmas Eve! in the Palace where knavery
Crowds all the treasures the fair world can render;
Where spirits grow rusted in silkenest slavery,
And life is out-panted, in sloth, and in splendour;
In gladness and glory, Wealth's darlings were meeting,
And jewel-claspt fingers linkt softly again;
New friendships were twining, and old friends were greeting,
And twin hearts grew one, in God's golden love-chain.

Merry Christmas Eve ! in a poor man's grim hovel,
There huddled in silence a famishing family ;
Church-bells were laughing in musical revel,
They heard the loud mockery, withnbrows throbbing clammily ;
All in the merry time there they sat, mourning—
Two sons—two brothers—in penal chains bleeding ;
Their hearts wandered forth to the never-returning,
Who rose on their vision, pale, haggard, and pleading.

Merry Christmas Eve ! for the rich, as in duty,
Taste pander'd and ruby wine woo'd on the board,
Eyes smiled in feign'd glory, on birth, and on beauty ;
And lying lips flatter'd the Mammonite lord.
Love-kisses sobb'd out, 'twixt the rollic and rout,
And Hope went forth, reaping-in long-promist treasure.
What matter, tho' hearts might be breaking without?
Their groans were unheard in the palace of pleasure.

Merry Christmas Eve ! but the stricken ones heard
No neighbourly welcome, no kind voice of kin ;
They lookt at each other, but spake not a word,
While through crevice, and cranny, the sleet drifted in,
In a desolate corner, one, hunger-kill'd, lay,
And the mother's hot tears were the bosom-babe's food
What marvel, O Statesmen, what marvel, I pray,
Such misery nurseth Crime's dark viper-brood ?

O men, angel-imaged in Nature's fair mint,
  And is it for this, ye were fashioned divine ?
Ah, where's the god-stamp—Immortality's print ?
  We are tyrants and slaves, knit in one tortured twine :
That a few, like to gods, may stride over the earth,
  Millions, born to heart-murder, are given in pawn ,
When will the world quicken for Liberty's birth,
  Which she waiteth, with eager wings beating the dawn ?

False Priest, dare ye say 'tis the will of your God
  (And shroud the Christ's message in dark sophistry),
That these millions of paupers should bow to the sod ?
  Up, up, trampled hearts, it's a lie ! it's a lie !
They may carve "State" and "Altar" in characters golden,
  But Tyranny's symbols are ceasing to win ;
Be stirring, O people, your scroll is unfolden,
  And bright be the deeds ye emblazon therein.

---

## ALL'S RIGHT WITH THE WORLD.

Sweet Phosphor tricks to a smile the brow of heaven,
Dawn's golden springs surge into floods of day,
Lush-leavy woods break into singing, Earth
From dewy dark rolls round her balmy side,
And all goes right, and merrily, with the world.

Spring with a tender beauty clothes the Earth,
Happy, and jewelled like a sumptuous Bride,
As tho' she knew no sorrow—held no grave :
No glory dims for all the hearts that break,
And all goes right, and merrily, with the world.

Birds sing as sweetly on the blossom'd boughs,
Suns mount as royally their sapphire throne,
Stars bud in gorgeous gloom, and harvests yield,
As tho' man nestled in the lap of Love :
All, all goes right, and merrily, with the world.

But slip this silken-folded mask aside,
And lo, Hell welters at our very feet !
The Poor are murder'd body and soul, the Rich
In Pleasure's chalice melt their pearl of life !
Ay, all goes right, and merrily, with the world.

Lean out into the looming Future, mark
The battle roll across the night to come !
"See how we right our Wrongs at last," Revenge
Writes with red radiance on the midnight heaven :
Yet, all goes right, and merrily, with the world.

So Sodom, grim old Reveller ! went to death.
Voluptuous Music throbb'd thro' all her courts,

Mirth wanton'd at her heart, one pulse before
Fire-tongues told out her bloody tale of wrong,—
And all went right, and merrily, with the world.

---

## BRIDAL SONG.

Gaily the Sun woos the Spring for his Bride
   With kisses all warm and golden ;
Till the life at her heart she no longer may hide,
   And the wealth of her lover is unfolden.

With kisses, sweet kisses, the mellow Rains start
   The virgin flowers a-blossom :
And ripen their beauty till fragrant lips part,
   And Love's jewel gleams rich in their bosom.

Faint with love wingeth the wantoning Wind,
   And yearns as its heart were a-breaking,
And kisses sweet kisses, till buds be untwined ;
   And the young leaves all are awaking.

The wrinkled old Sea sidles up the sands,
   And lavishes kisses in showers
On the Earth, till the Grey-beard's young darling stands
   All dressed in her bridal flowers !

And there's nothing so dainty-sweet in life
  As to kiss the Maid, glowing and tender,
Till the heart of the Wife, giveth up in the strife,
  Full-flowering in Love's splendour.

---

## A CHAUNT.

EARTH like a Lover poor and low
Feasts on Night's queenly beauty now ;
While I, with burning heart and brow,
    Awake to weep for thee, Love !
The spangled glories of the Night,
The Moon that walks in soft, white light,
These cannot win my charméd sight,
    Or lure a thought from thee, Love !

I'm thinking o'er the short, sweet hour,
Our hearts drank up Love's growth of power,
And summer'd as in Eden's bower,
    When I was blest with thee, Love !
There burn'd no beauty on the trees,
There woke no song of birds or bees,
But Love's cup for us held no lees,
    And I was blest with thee, Love.

Then grand and golden fancies spring
From out my heart, on splendid wing,
Like Chrysalis from Life's wintering—
    Burst bright and summeringly, Love !
And as a Chief of battle lost
Counts, and recounts, his stricken host,
Stands tearful Memory making most
    Of all that's toucht with thee, Love.

Perchance in Pleasure's brilliant bower
Thy heart may half forget Love's power,
But at this still and starry hour
    Does it not turn to me, Love ?
O, by all pangs for thy sweet sake,
In my deep love thy heart-thirst slake,
Or, all-too-full, my heart must break :
    Break ! break ! with loving thee, Love !

---

## SONG.

O lay thy hand in mine, dear !
  We're growing old, We're growing old ;
But Time hath wrought no sign, dear,
  That hearts grow cold, that hearts grow cold.

'Tis long, long since our new love
  Made life divine, made life divine ;
But age enricheth true love,
  Like noble wine, like noble wine.

O lay thy cheek to mine, dear,
  And take thy rest, and take thy rest ;
Mine arms around thee twine, dear,
  And make thy nest, and make thy nest.
A many cares are pressing
  On this dear head, on this dear head ;
But Sorrow's hands in blessing
  Are surely laid, are surely laid.

O lean thy life on mine, dear!
  'Twill shelter thee, 'twill shelter thee.
Thou wert a winsome vine, dear,
  On my young tree, on my young tree :
And so, till boughs are leafless,
  And Song-birds flown, and Song-birds flown,
We'll twine ; then lay us, griefless,
  Together down, together down.

## ENGLAND GOES TO BATTLE.

Now, glory to our England,
  As she rises, calm and grand,
With the ancient spirit in her eyes,—
  The good Sword in her hand !
Our royal right on battle-ground,
  Was aye to bear the brunt :
Ho ! brave heart ! for one passionate bound,
  And take thy place in front !
Now glory to our England,
  As she rises, calm and grand,
With the ancient spirit in her eyes—
  The good Sword in her hand !

Who would not fight for England ?
  Who would not fling a life
I' the ring, to meet a Tyrant's gage,
  And glory in the strife ?
Her stem is thorny, but doth burst
  A glorious Rose a-top !
And shall our dear Rose wither ?  First
  We'll drain life's dearest drop !

Who would not fight for England?
  Who would not fling a life
I' the ring, to meet a Tyrant's gage,
  And glory in the strife?

To battle goes our England,
  All as gallant and as gay
As Lover to the Altar, on
  A merry marriage-day.
A weary night she stood to watch
  The battle-dawn up-roll'd;
And her spirit leaps within, to match
  The noble deeds of old.
To battle goes our England,
  All as gallant and as gay
As Lover to the Altar, on
  A merry marriage-day.

Now, fair befall our England,
  On her proud and perilous road;
And woe and wail to those who make
  Her foot-prints red with blood!
Up with our red-cross banner—roll
  A thunder-peal of drums!
Fight on there, every valiant soul,
  And courage! England comes!

Now, fair befall our England,
  On her proud and perilous road:
And woe and wail to those who make
  Her foot-prints red with blood!

Now, victory to our England!
  And where'er she lifts her hand
In Freedom's fight, to rescue Right,
  God bless the dear Old Land!
And when the Storm has pass'd away,
  In glory and in calm,
May she sit down, i' the green o' the day,
  And sing her peaceful psalm!
Now, victory to our England!
  And where'er she lifts her hand
In Freedom's fight, to rescue Right,
  God bless the dear Old Land!

THE END.

www.ingramcontent.com/pod-product-compliance
Lightning Source LLC
LaVergne TN
LVHW050524100826
845148LV00002B/430

* 9 7 8 1 4 2 5 5 2 0 7 2 4 *